Deliciously Vintage

Deliciously Vintage

Sixty beloved cakes and bakes
that stand the test of time

Victoria Glass

RYLAND PETERS & SMALL
LONDON • NEW YORK

Senior Designer Megan Smith
Designer Maria Lee-Warren
Commissioning Editor
Stephanie Milner
Head of Production
Patricia Harrington
Art Director Leslie Harrington
Editorial Director Julia Charles

Food Stylist Bridget Sargeson
Assistant Food Stylist
Laura Urschel
Prop Stylist Tony Hutchinson
Indexer Hilary Bird

First published in 2014 by
Ryland Peters & Small
20–21 Jockey's Fields, London
WC1R 4BW
and
519 Broadway, 5th Floor,
New York, NY 10012
www.rylandpeters.com
10 9 8 7 6 5 4 3 2 1

Text © Victoria Glass 2014
Design and photographs
© Ryland Peters & Small 2014

Printed in China.

ISBN: 978-1-84975-486-6

A CIP record for this book is
available from the British Library.
US Library of Congress
cataloging-in-Publication Data
has been applied for.

Notes

• All spoon measurements are
level unless otherwise specified.
• All eggs are medium (UK) or
large (US), unless specified as
large, in which case US extra-
large should be used. Uncooked
or partially cooked eggs should
not be served to the very old,
frail, young children, pregnant
women or those with
compromised immune systems.

• When a recipe calls for the
grated zest of citrus fruit, buy
unwaxed fruit and wash well
before using. If you can only find
treated fruit, scrub well in warm
soapy water before using.
• When a recipe calls for full-fat
cream cheese, it should be white,
creamy smooth and have at least
24 per cent fat content, such as
Kraft Philadelphia.
• Ovens should be preheated
to the specified temperatures.
We recommend using an oven
thermometer. If using a fan-
assisted oven, adjust temperatures
according to the manufacturer's
instructions.
• To sterilize preserving jars, wash
them in hot, soapy water and
rinse in boiling water. Place in
a large saucepan and cover with
hot water. With the saucepan lid
on, bring the water to a boil and
continue boiling for 15 minutes.
Turn off the heat and leave the
jars in the hot water until just
before they are to be filled.
Invert the jars onto a clean dish
towel to dry. Sterilize the lids
for 5 minutes, by boiling or
according to the manufacturer's
instructions. Jars should be filled
and sealed while they are still hot.

Contents

Introduction

There is nothing quite so evocative of childhood and happiness as the welcoming smell of freshly made cakes, buns and biscuits. Baking nurtures the senses, enveloping us in its intoxicating aroma like a soft blanket on a cold day.

At the beginning of Marcel Proust's classic novel, *In Search of Lost Time*, the narrator is whisked off into his memories by the bite of a simple madeleine, dunked in a cup of hot tea. It is no coincidence that Proust chose a dainty little cake as the catalyst for this poetic reminiscence, rather than have the narrator tuck into a bowl of tripe and onions.

Home baking is about warmth and generosity of spirit. We bake for those we love to show support in times of need, to celebrate in times of success and to watch children's faces light up at the sight of delicate wings on butterfly cakes and oozing jam peeking from the cut-out hearts of jammie dodgers.

The first bake I learned to make was at my mother's knee and it was, along with most British children, I suspect, a Victoria sponge. The smell of vanilla cake filling the kitchen still brings back strong memories of my childhood home, standing on a chair so I could peer into the oven door, while repeating with eager frequency, 'Is it nearly ready yet?' and 'What about... now?'

There are so many different bakes that are redolent of particular times in my life. Black Forest gâteau brings me back to afternoons watching the Saturday matinee on television when it was raining. Bakewell tart reminds me of winter, because my grandmother fed me a slice when I was sent home from school early because of the snow. Crumbles kindle memories of my sisters and I foraging for blackberries and using the hooked arms of umbrellas to draw forward the ripest fruits at the top of the bramble bushes. Almost every cake, biscuit, cookie and pudding comes with a connection to happy times past, from learning to bake to the thrill of the anticipation in waiting for them to come out of the oven and, finally, to the pleasure in eating and sharing them. Baking's link with nostalgia, compassion and hospitality will always ensure its appeal endures.

I felt it would be useful to offer a few notes to my American readers on the eccentricities of the British baking vocabulary: 'biscuit' is generally synonymous in the UK with the 'cookie', although cookies are often softer in texture than traditional British biscuits. Scones in British English share similarities with American biscuits, but are usually sweet and served with cream and jam, never gravy. We also, and perhaps most confusingly, tend to

use the words 'pudding' and 'dessert' interchangeably, whether we are eating something that has pudding in its title (such as the Sticky Toffee Pudding on page 132) or not.

Many recipes in this collection of vintage bakes will already be familiar to you and perhaps already be a part of

your baking repertoire, but I hope to inspire you to discover more favourite bakes and create new memories along the way.

Victoria
xo

Baking Basics

There are techniques that crop up again and again in baking and once you've mastered the basics you can make any cake, bake, slice, pudding or tart. Some recipes call for ingredients that are readily available to buy but if you want to go all-out, here are the recipes you need to make your own.

Techniques

Kneading

To 'knead' means to stretch and move dough with your hands. The reason this is important is so the gluten in the flour develops to create elasticity and a good-textured bake. In most recipes you will need to knead for at least 5 minutes, but more likely 10, by hand. Alternatively, you can use a freestanding mixer with a dough hook attachment.

Proving

Proving (sometimes known as 'proofing') happens during the resting time after the dough has been kneaded when the yeast feeds on the dough causing it to rise. Most yeast doughs require two proving/rising times.

'Knock back'

Knocking back removes the air pockets out of the risen dough to create an even texture before a second proving. Simply form a fist and force it straight down into the centre of your risen dough. Then fold the dough back in on itself and gently knead it for another minute or so before shaping the dough and covering it for a second proving.

Tempering chocolate

Tempering is simply a heating and cooling process at controlled temperatures to ensure the crystals in chocolate remain as small and stable as possible, so that the chocolate has a lovely 'snap' and retains its gloss. Tempering is essential to prevent your chocolate from 'blooming' – the white, matte streaks sometimes seen on chocolate. The easiest method is the seeding method. You will need a chocolate thermometer to ensure complete accuracy.

Finely chop your chocolate, place two-thirds in a heatproof bowl suspended over a pan of barely simmering water to melt gently. You can give it a stir with a rubber spatula every now and then to help move things along. Make sure the bottom of your bowl does not touch the water or your chocolate may seize.

Once the chocolate has melted, remove the bowl from the heat and add the remaining chocolate. Put your chocolate thermometer into the cooling chocolate and stir continuously until it reaches 31–32°C (89–90°F) for dark/bittersweet chocolate, 29–30°C (84–86°F) for milk/semisweet chocolate, or 28–29°C (82–84°F) for white chocolate. Your chocolate is now tempered and ready to use.

Blind baking

Blind baking simply means to pre-bake a pastry case before the filling is added. It is necessary when the filling takes less time to bake than the pastry, but also ensures a crisp base to prevent soggy bottoms. Once the tart pan has been lined with pastry, simply place a sheet of baking parchment over the top and fill the pastry case with baking beans, rice or dried beans or pulses. The pastry is then blind baked for the specified time before the baking beans and paper is removed and the pastry case can be filled.

Homemade Ingredients

Cream Cheese Frosting

200 g/6½ oz. full-fat
   cream cheese
125 g/1 stick unsalted
   butter, softened
500 g/3⅓ cups
   icing/confectioners'
   sugar

2 teaspoons pure vanilla
   extract
finely grated zest of
   1 lemon

makes single quantity

To make the frosting, whisk the cream cheese and butter together in a large mixing bowl until light and fluffy. Sift over half of the icing/confectioners' sugar and whisk again until combined. Sift over the remaining icing/confectioners' sugar and whisk again. Whisk in the vanilla and lemon zest until the frosting is light, fluffy and spreadable.

Meringue

5 egg whites
a pinch of salt
250 g/1¼ cups caster/
   superfine sugar
2 teaspoons cornflour/
   cornstarch

1 teaspoon lemon juice/
   white wine vinegar

makes single quantity

To make the meringue, whisk the egg whites and salt together in a large bowl until stiff and gradually, 1 tablespoon at a time, add the sugar, whisking well between each addition. Once all the sugar has been incorporated, add the cornflour/cornstarch and lemon juice and whisk again.

Royal Icing

1 large fresh egg white
325 g/13 oz icing/
   confectioners' sugar

freshly squeezed juice
   of ½–1 lemon

makes single quantity

Royal icing is the key ingredient for piping pretty designs. It also makes the perfect edible glue for sticking on sweets.

Whisk the egg white in a large mixing bowl until light and fluffy then sift in the icing/confectioners' sugar. Whisk again and add the lemon juice.

When piping, it is always best to use royal icing on the day it has been made. If the use of raw egg white concerns you, you can substitute it for powdered egg white – follow the manufacturer's instructions for quantities.

Sugar Glaze

2 tablespoons caster/
   granulated sugar
2 tablespoons whole
   milk

makes single quantity

Put the sugar and milk together in a pan and stir over a gentle heat until the sugar has dissolved. Stop stirring and bring to the boil. Simmer for a few minutes until the glaze has reduced and thickened.

Toffee Sauce

200 g/1 cup light
   muscovado sugar
100 g/½ cup dark
   muscovado sugar
60 g/5 tablespoons
   butter
4 tablespoons golden/
   light corn syrup

1 tablespoon pure
   vanilla extract
¼ teaspoon salt
250 ml/1 cup double/
   heavy cream

makes single quantity

Put all the ingredients, except for the cream, into a saucepan and stir over a gentle heat until all the sugar has dissolved. Bring to a rolling boil, before stirring in the cream and removing from the heat.

Accompaniments

Custard sauce

5 egg yolks
50 g/¼ cup caster/granulated sugar
**2 vanilla pods/beans, halved and
seeds removed**
250 ml/1 cup whole milk
250 ml/1 cup single/light cream

serves 4

Whisk the egg yolks and sugar together in a large heatproof bowl until pale and thickened, then put a sieve/strainer over the top.

In the meantime, put the vanilla pods/beans and seeds, milk and cream into a large saucepan over a gentle heat. When the mixture just begins to boil, remove from the heat and pour over the egg mixture through the sieve, then whisk thoroughly (remove and discard the vanilla pods).

Return the custard to the saucepan (you can quickly rinse it out first, if you want to) and place over a gentle heat. Stir continuously until the custard is thick enough to coat the back of a spoon and pour into a cold jug/pitcher to prevent it cooking any further.

Marzipan

1 egg
1 egg yolk
250 g/2 cups icing/
   confectioners' sugar,
   plus extra to dust

1 teaspoon lemon juice
1 tablespoon brandy
250 g/1^2/$_3$ cups ground
   almonds

makes single quantity

Put the egg and egg yolk and icing/confectioners' sugar in a large heatproof bowl set over a pan of barely simmering water. Whisk continuously with a balloon or electric hand whisk until the mixture is pale, thick and doubled in volume. Make sure you keep the heat low or the mixture will curdle. Whisk in the lemon juice and brandy until thoroughly combined, then take the bowl off the heat and leave to cool. Whisk again, pour in the ground almonds and stir to combine, then knead to form a firm dough. Wrap in clingfilm/plastic wrap and leave to rest for at least 2 hours before rolling out on a surface dusted with icing/confectioners' sugar.

Fruit Jam/Jelly

1 kg/8 cups fresh fruit
   of your choosing
   (I use hulled
   strawberries here)
1 kg/5 cups jam/jelly
   sugar

freshly squeezed juice
   of 1 lemon
waxed paper
sterilized jars
   (see page 4)

makes 500 ml/2 cups

Before you start, put a saucer in the freezer. Chop a handful of the strawberries into large chunks, or leave whole if small, and set aside. Put the remaining strawberries in a large, wide saucepan and mash with a potato masher into a rough pulp. Stir in the sugar and lemon juice and place over a gentle heat. Stir until the sugar has dissolved and increase the heat to bring to the boil for 3 minutes before adding the remaining strawberries. Continue to boil for a further 6 minutes, stirring every now and then and skim off any pink scum off the top with a slotted spoon.

Remove the pan from the heat and put a small dollop of jam on to the chilled saucer. When the jam is cold, run your finger over it and if it wrinkles, the jam is set. If you have a sugar/candy thermometer, the setting point for jam is 104.5°C/220°F. Decant the jam into the sterilized jars (see page 4), put a disc of waxed paper on top of each and tightly screw on their lids.

Vanilla Ice Cream

4 egg yolks
100 g/^{1}/$_2$ cup caster/
   granulated sugar
2 vanilla pods
350 ml/1^1/$_3$ cups
   double/heavy cream

an ice cream maker
   (optional)

serves 4

Whisk the egg yolks and sugar together in a large heatproof bowl until pale and thickened, then put a sieve/strainer over the top.

In the meantime, split the vanilla pods and scrape out the seeds. Put the cream and vanilla pods and seeds into a large saucepan set over a gentle heat. When the mixture just begins to boil, remove from the heat, pour over the egg mixture through the sieve and whisk thoroughly (discard the vanilla pods).

Return the custard to the saucepan (you can quickly rinse it out first, if you want to) and place over a gentle heat. Stir continuously until the custard is thick enough to coat the back of a spoon and pour into a cold jug/pitcher to prevent it cooking any further. Put a sheet of clingfilm/plastic wrap over the top to prevent a skin forming and leave to cool completely.

Transfer the custard to the fridge for 1 hour before pouring into an ice cream maker and following the manufacturer's instructions. If you do not have an ice cream maker, you can transfer the custard into a freezerproof, plastic container and put it in the freezer, though you must give it a vigorous whisk every 30 minutes to prevent ice crystals forming. The ice cream should be completely set within 3–4 hours.

Biscuits & Cookies

Jammie Dodgers

Named after Roger the Dodger from *The Beano* comics, Jammie Dodgers are one of the UK's favourite treats, and for very good reason. Perfect for dunking and adored by young and old, these crumbly shortbread sandwiches are generously filled with seedless raspberry jam that invitingly peeks through a heart-shaped hole.

250 g/2 sticks unsalted butter, softened
125 g/²⁄₃ cup caster/granulated sugar
275 g/2 cups plus 2 tablespoons plain/all-purpose flour
100 g/³⁄₄ cup rice flour
a pinch of salt
2 teaspoons pure vanilla extract

250 g/8 oz. seedless raspberry jam/jelly (see page 11)
2 baking sheets, lined with baking parchment
a 6-cm/2½-in. round, crinkle/fluted cookie cutter
a 2.5-cm/1-in. heart-shaped cookie cutter

makes 15

Cream together the butter and sugar in a large bowl until light and fluffy. Sift over the flours and salt and mix together with the pure vanilla extract until just combined. Do not overwork the dough or the biscuits will be tough. Chill the dough for at least 30 minutes in the fridge.

Roll out the dough on a lightly floured surface to ½ cm/¼ inch thick and cut out 30 rounds with the round cutter. Using the heart-shaped cutter, cut out a heart-shaped hole in the centre of half of the biscuits and then put all the biscuits on the prepared baking sheets. Chill them for 1 hour in the fridge.

Preheat the oven to 160°C (325°F) Gas 3.

Remove the biscuits from the fridge and bake for 15–20 minutes. Transfer to a wire rack and let cool completely. To assemble, place a rounded teaspoon of jam on each whole biscuit and press a biscuit with a heart-shaped window on top.

Jumbles

Jumbles are little knot-shaped biscuits which were popular in Tudor England. I have adapted a recipe from Thomas Dawson's *The Good Huswifes Jewell* dated 1596, in which he uses the archaic spelling 'iombles'. Dawson specifies the inclusion of rose water, mace and caraway, but I have also added grated lemon zest for freshness and zing.

100 g/6½ tablespoons
   unsalted butter
100 g/½ cup caster/
   granulated sugar
2 eggs
a generous splash
   of rose water
a pinch of salt
1 teaspoon ground
   mace
3 teaspoons caraway
   seeds
finely grated zest of
   1 unwaxed lemon
200 g/1⅔ cups plain/
   all-purpose flour

*2 baking sheets,
   lined with baking
   parchment*

makes 18–20

Preheat the oven to 180°C (350°F) Gas 4. Beat the butter and sugar together in a large bowl until light and fluffy. Gradually beat in the eggs and add the rose water. Stir in the salt, spices and lemon zest, then add the flour. Mix together thoroughly to make a fairly stiff dough. Add a little water to bring the dough together if you need to.

Roll out the dough on a lightly floured surface into a long sausage about 1.5 cm/¾ in. wide and cut it into approximately 8-cm/3½-in. pieces. Tie each piece into a knot shape, then transfer to the prepared baking sheets and bake for 12–15 minutes. Transfer to a wire rack to cool

Chocolate Chip Cookies

Invented by Ruth Wakefield of the Toll House Inn in Whitman, Massachusetts in the 1930s, chocolate chip cookies have remained firm family favourites ever since. Sweet, buttery and studded with nibs of dark/bittersweet chocolate, these cookies are perfect dunked into a glass of cold milk or a cup of hot, milky tea.

125 g/1 stick unsalted butter, softened

75 g/⅓ cup light brown sugar

75 g/⅓ cup caster/granulated sugar

1 egg

2 teaspoons pure vanilla extract

250 g/2 cups plain/all-purpose flour

1 teaspoon bicarbonate of soda/baking soda

½ teaspoon salt

175 g/6 oz. dark/bittersweet chocolate chips

2 baking sheets, lined with baking parchment

makes about 20

Cream together the butter and sugars in a large bowl until just combined.

Beat in the egg, followed by the pure vanilla extract.

Sift over the flour, bicarbonate of soda/baking soda and salt, then mix in. Fold in the chocolate chips last.

Wrap the dough in clingfilm/plastic wrap and chill in the fridge for at least 2 hours before baking.

Preheat the oven to 180°C (350°F) Gas 4.

Roll the chilled cookie dough with your hands into golf ball-size rounds and space them well apart on the prepared baking sheets.

Slightly flatten each ball with either a palette knife or the base of your palm.

Bake for 12–15 minutes, or until slightly golden. Transfer them to a wire rack to cool.

I enjoyed many family holidays in Cornwall, in the south west of England, as a child, where we would joyfully scoff Cornish fairings with a pot of tea. They are called fairings because traditionally they were bought as gifts at Cornish fairs. In fact, anything from a fair was considered a 'fairing', but the name has stuck for these wonderful, spiced Cornish treats.

Cornish Fairings

100 g/³⁄₄ cup plain/
  all-purpose flour
½ teaspoon
  bicarbonate of soda/
  baking soda
½ teaspoon baking
  powder
1 teaspoon ground
  ginger
1 teaspoon mixed/apple
  pie spice
¼ teaspoon ground
  cinnamon
50 g/¼ cup light
  muscovado sugar
a pinch of salt
50 g/3 tablespoons cold
  unsalted butter, cut
  into cubes
2 tablespoons golden/
  light corn syrup

*2 baking sheets, lined
  with baking
  parchment.*

makes about 24

Preheat the oven to 180°C (350°F) Gas 4.

Sift the flour, bicarbonate of soda/baking soda, baking powder and spices into a large bowl. Add the sugar, salt and butter and rub the mixture with your fingertips until it resembles fine breadcrumbs. Warm the syrup in a small saucepan over a gentle heat, then stir it through the mixture to make a soft dough.

Roll the dough into walnut-size balls with your hands and place on the prepared baking sheets with room for spreading in between.

Bake for 7–8 minutes and take the baking sheets out of the oven. Give each baking sheet a good whack on a solid surface to make the biscuits crack and return to the oven for a further 4–5 minutes or until evenly golden. Be careful not to overbake the biscuits or they will be too hard and crisp. Transfer to a wire rack to cool.

Gingerbread Men

Gingerbread men date back to the 16th century, when Queen Elizabeth I had gingerbread figures made in the likeness of her guests. These days, gingerbread men are still favoured by adults and children alike and are often adorned with sweets, dried fruits, icing and chocolate to depict faces, hats and coat buttons.

85 g/scant ½ cup dark muscovado sugar

3 tablespoons clear runny honey

2 tablespoons ground ginger

½ teaspoon salt

1 tablespoon pure vanilla extract

100 g/6½ tablespoons unsalted butter, cut into cubes

½ teaspoon bicarbonate of soda/ baking soda

225 g/1¾ cups plain/ all-purpose flour

To decorate

1 quantity royal icing (see page 9)

a handful of sweets or sugar sprinkles

an 8-cm/3½-inch gingerbread man cookie cutter

2 baking sheets, lined with baking parchment

makes 18–20

Put the dark muscovado sugar, honey, ground ginger, salt and pure vanilla extract into a saucepan over a medium heat. Stir until all the sugar has dissolved, stop stirring and bring to the boil.

Remove the pan from the heat and stir in the cubes of butter until melted. Add the bicarbonate of soda/ baking soda and mix. Transfer to a large bowl and allow to cool slightly.

Sift over the flour and combine thoroughly. Set aside to cool. Once completely cold, wrap the dough in clingfilm/plastic wrap and put it in the fridge for 2–3 hours.

When ready to bake, preheat the oven to 200°C (400°F) Gas 6.

Gently knead the dough before rolling it to ½ cm/¼ inch thick between two sheets of clingfilm/ plastic wrap – this stops the dough from sticking to the work surface without the need for extra flour.

Stamp out the biscuits/cookies using the cutter and carefully transfer to the prepared baking sheets. Put the gingerbread back in the fridge for 30 minutes before baking – this will help to keep an even shape.

Bake for 8–10 minutes or until just firm to the touch.

Remove the gingerbread men from the oven and cool on a wire rack before decorating with royal icing and sweets.

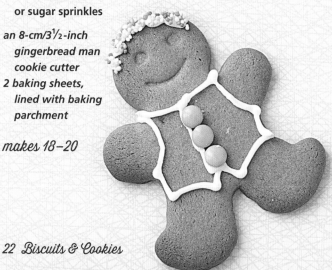

Florentine Biscuits

These chewy Italian treats are impressively showy, but deceptively easy to make. Perfect for an afternoon lift or as indulgent *petit fours* served with coffee after dinner. They work wonderfully with different spices, fruits and nuts to suit all occasions and moods; substitute dried cranberries for the cherries at Christmas for a lovely festive change. Versatile and sophisticated, these are innocent-looking but highly addictive. You have been warned!

50 g/3 tablespoons unsalted butter

100 ml/scant ½ cup double/heavy cream

125 g/⅔ cup light muscovado sugar

2 tablespoons clear runny honey

50 g/½ cup glacé/candied cherries, chopped

140 g/1 cup desiccated/shredded coconut

125 g/1¼ cups flaked/slivered almonds

50 g/⅓ cup Chinese stem (candied) ginger in syrup, finely chopped

50 g/⅓ cup mixed candied peel

50 g/⅓ cup plus 1 tablespoon plain/all-purpose flour, sifted

a pinch of salt

125 g/4 oz. dark/bittersweet chocolate

2 large baking sheets, lined with baking parchment

makes about 30

Preheat the oven to 180°C (350°F) Gas 4.

Put the butter, cream sugar and honey in a saucepan set over a gentle heat. Stir until the sugar has dissolved and bring to the boil. Take the pan off the heat and vigorously stir in the remaining ingredients except for the chocolate. Leave the mixture to cool for a few minutes.

Dollop generous teaspoons of mixture at 5-cm/2-in. intervals on to the prepared baking sheets and flatten each one with the back of a spoon. They will spread further on baking. Bake for 8–10 minutes or until golden. Leave to cool completely on a wire rack.

Finely chop the chocolate and put ⅔ in a heatproof bowl over a pan of barely simmering water. Once the chocolate has completely melted, take the bowl of the heat and stir in the remaining chocolate with a rubber spatula until all the chocolate has melted.

Use a pastry brush to generously paint the Florentines with chocolate. If the chocolate isn't thick enough, you can paint each one with a second coat; by the time you have painted the first coat on the last Florentine, the first Florentine should have set enough for a second coat. Allow the chocolate to cool and set before serving.

Millionaire's Shortbread

For the shortbread

75 g/6 tablespoons
caster/granulated
sugar

150 g/10 tablespoons
unsalted butter,
softened

125 g/1 cup plain/
all-purpose flour

100 g/³/₄ cup rice flour

a generous pinch of salt

2 teaspoons pure vanilla
extract

For the caramel

125 g/1 stick unsalted
butter

75 g/6 tablespoons light
muscovado sugar

25 g/1 tablespoon plus
2 teaspoons golden/
light corn syrup

1 tablespoon pure
vanilla extract

a pinch of salt

1 x 379 g/14 oz. can
(sweetened)
condensed milk

200 g/6½ oz.
dark/semisweet
chocolate, broken
into pieces

20-cm/8-in. square
loose-bottomed/
springform cake pan,
greased and lined
with baking
parchment

makes 16

Sticky, sweet and deliciously indulgent, this traybake can't fail to hit the spot. Shortbread dates back to Elizabethan-era Scotland, the millionaire layers of caramel and chocolate being a more recent addition, believed to have been introduced in the 19th century.

Preheat the oven to 150°C (300°F) Gas 2.

Cream together the sugar and butter in a large bowl until light and fluffy. Sift over the flours and mix together with the salt and vanilla extract until just combined. Do not overwork the dough or the shortbread will be tough.

Press the dough in the base of the cake pan with your fingers or using the back of a spoon and bake for 45–50 minutes. Leave to cool in the pan on a wire rack.

Meanwhile, make the caramel topping. Put all the ingredients, except for the condensed milk, into a saucepan or pot and stir over a gentle heat until the butter has melted and the sugar has dissolved. Add the (sweetened) condensed milk and increase the heat, stirring frequently, being careful not to let the base of the mixture catch. Bring to the boil, still stirring every now and then, until the mixture has thickened and turned a deep golden colour. Remove from the heat and leave to cool slightly. Pour the warm caramel over the cooled shortbread base and leave to cool completely.

Put the chocolate in a heatproof bowl set over a saucepan or pot of barely simmering water to melt. Stir every now and then. Once melted, leave to cool slightly before pouring the chocolate over the cold caramel. Leave to cool completely before pushing the base of the pan out and cutting the millionaire's shortbread into 16 squares.

Black & White Cookies

These giant New York cookies are half black and half white, like a half moon in a night sky. They are iconic thanks to an episode of the hit US show, *Seinfeld*, in which they were used as a metaphor for racial harmony, before being dubbed 'unity cookies' by Barack Obama. Soft and cakey in texture, they are light and subtle in fragrance, despite their ostentatious appearance.

For the cookies
150 g/1 stick plus 2 tablespoons unsalted butter, softened
175 g/3/4 cup plus 2 tablespoons caster/granulated sugar
2 eggs
315 g/2½ cups plain/all-purpose flour
1 teaspoon bicarbonate of soda/baking soda
1 teaspoon salt
1 tablespoon pure vanilla extract
finely grated zest of 1 lemon
175 ml/3/4 cups buttermilk

For the icing
1 egg white
200 g/1²/3 cups icing/confectioners' sugar, sifted
2 teaspoons pure vanilla extract
150 g/5 oz. dark/bittersweet chocolate, melted and cooled

3 baking sheets, lined with parchment paper

makes 15

Preheat the oven to 180°C (350°F) Gas 4.

To make the cookies, cream together the butter and sugar in a large bowl, then whisk in the eggs. Sift together the flour, bicarbonate of soda/baking soda and salt in a separate bowl. Stir the vanilla and lemon zest into the buttermilk in a glass measuring cup/jug. Alternately whisk in ⅓ of the dry ingredients, then ⅓ of the buttermilk mixture into the butter mixture. Repeat until all the ingredients are fully incorporated.

Drop 1 rounded tablespoon of batter in a mound on to one of the prepared baking sheets, before flattening it into a neat circle with a palette knife. Repeat, leaving a 4-cm/2-in. gap between each cookie.

Bake for 15–20 minutes or until the cookies have slightly coloured. Transfer to a wire rack to cool.

For the icing, whisk the egg white, icing/confectioners' sugar and vanilla extract

together until you have a thick, glossy icing. You may need to make the icing thinner with a few drops of water, but add only a little at a time.

Use a palette knife to spread half of each cookie with the icing on one side and leave to set. Once the icing is set, spread the other half of each cookie with the melted chocolate. Leave the cookies to set before serving.

Snickerdoodles

300 g/1½ cups caster/
granulated sugar
225 g/15 tablespoons
unsalted butter,
softened
2 eggs
345 g/2⅔ cups plain/
all-purpose flour
2 teaspoons cream of
tartar
1 teaspoon baking
powder
¼ teaspoon salt

*For the cinnamon
coating*
50 g/¼ cup caster/
granulated sugar
3 teaspoons ground
cinnamon

*2 large baking sheets,
lined with baking
parchment*

makes about 60

Preheat oven to 200°C (400°F) Gas 6 .

Cream the sugar and butter together in a large
bowl until pale and fluffy. Gradually whisk in the
eggs and sift over the flour, cream of tartar, baking
powder and salt. Mix until the mixture starts to
come together, then use your hands to bring the
mixture together to form a dough. Put the cookie
dough in the fridge for 30 minutes to firm up.

Dust your hands with flour and roll the dough
between your hands into hazelnut-size pieces.
Mix together the sugar and cinnamon in a
shallow bowl and roll each ball in the sugar
until thoroughly coated. Place the balls of dough
on to the baking sheets with about 5 cm/2 in.
between each one. Flatten each ball slightly with
a palette knife.

Bake for 10–12 minutes, or until firm. Leave the
cookies to cool for 5 minutes before transferring
them to a wire rack to cool completely.

It's not just their name that makes these American cookies memorable. Sweet and fragrant with cinnamon, these sweet treats are crisp on the outside with soft, chewy centres. Simple to make, these cookies are such a crowd-pleaser that you will want to bake them again and again.

Anzac Biscuits

This Antipodean biscuit is a popular fundraising bake for ANZAC Day, thanks to its connection with the Australian and New Zealand Army Corps, despite recent evidence, which suggests that the Anzac biscuit, in its current form at least, was not known by this name until a year after World War I had ended. Regardless of their historical roots, oaty Anzac biscuits are delicious and chewy and perfect for dunking in a cuppa.

125 g/1 cup plain/ all-purpose flour

75 g/1 cup shredded/desiccated unsweetened coconut

75 g/²⁄₃ cup porridge/ old-fashioned rolled oats

150 g/³⁄₄ cup light muscovado sugar

a pinch of salt

125 g/1 stick unsalted butter

2 tablespoons golden/ light corn syrup

1 teaspoon bicarbonate of soda/baking soda

2 baking sheets, lined with baking parchment.

makes about 12

Preheat the oven to 160°C (325°F) Gas 3.

Sift the flour and bicarbonate of soda/baking soda into a large bowl and stir in the coconut, oats, sugar and salt. Put the butter, syrup and 2 tablespoons water in a saucepan over a medium heat and stir until all melted. Pour the butter mixture over the dry ingredients and mix together until thoroughly combined. Dollop generous teaspoonfuls of the mixture onto the prepared baking sheets, allowing enough room in between for spreading.

Bake for 8–10 minutes and transfer to a wire rack to cool.

Small Cakes & Bakes

Madeleine Cakes

Romanticized in the 'episode of the madeleine' in Proust's *In Search of Lost Time* for their connection with involuntary memory, these elegant French cakes are undeniably evocative. Delicate, light sponge, fragranced with lemon and served warm from the oven, madeleines are traditionally baked in shell-shaped moulds and are perfect dunked in a cup of hot tea.

100 g/½ cup caster/
  granulated sugar
2 eggs
100 g/6½ tablespoons
  unsalted butter,
  melted and cooled
  slightly
a pinch of salt
100 g/¾ cup plain/
  all-purpose flour
1 teaspoon baking
  powder
zest and juice of
  1 lemon
icing/confectioners'
  sugar, for dusting
  (optional)

a 12-shell madeleine
  pan, greased and
  floured

makes 12

In a large bowl, whisk together the granulated sugar and eggs until combined – the mixture should be light and frothy. Add the butter and salt, sift over the flour and baking powder, then lightly whisk to combine. Finally, stir through the lemon zest and juice and leave the batter to rest for at least 30 minutes.

Preheat the oven to 200°C (400°F) Gas 6.

Pour the batter into the prepared madeleine pan and bake for 8–10 minutes, or until each madeleine is slightly golden and well risen in the centre. Once the cakes have cooled enough to touch, transfer them to a wire rack to cool. Sift a little icing/confectioners' sugar over the madeleines before serving, if liked. Madeleines are best eaten on the day they are made.

The official state muffin of Minnesota, the
blueberry muffin has become as synonymous
with American breakfasts as the croissant
is with France. These sweet, yeast-free, quick
bread treats, studded with juicy blueberries,
are so easy to make and are delicious enough
to be enjoyed at any time of the day.

Blueberry Muffins

250 ml/1 cup buttermilk
100 g/6½ tablespoons
   unsalted butter,
   melted and cooled
   slightly
1 large egg, beaten
250 g/2 cups plain/
   all-purpose flour
1 teaspoon baking
   powder
1 teaspoon bicarbonate
   of soda/baking soda
200 g/1 cup caster/
   granulated sugar
a pinch of salt
200 g/1⅓ cups fresh
   blueberries

a 12-hole muffin pan,
   lined with paper cases

makes 12

Whisk together the buttermilk, melted butter and egg in a large glass measuring jug/cup. Sift together the flour, baking powder and bicarbonate of soda/baking soda in a large mixing bowl and add the sugar and salt. Pour the wet ingredients into the dry and use a fork to gently combine. Leave the batter to rest for at least 1 hour or in the fridge overnight.

Preheat the oven to 200°C (400°F) Gas 6.

Fold in the blueberries, divide the batter among the paper cases and bake for 20–25 minutes. Leave to cool slightly before tucking in.

Cream Buns

Who can resist a sweet bun filled with plenty of freshly whipped cream? This light, baked, doughnut-style bun is deliciously moreish. You can add a smear of raspberry or strawberry jam for some added fruity sweetness.

450 g/3½ cups plain/all-purpose flour

¾ teaspoon salt

40 g/2½ tablespoons cold butter, cut into cubes

225 ml/scant 1 cup whole milk

100 g/½ cup caster/granulated sugar

7 g/0.25 oz. sachet fast-action/rapid-rise yeast

1 egg

1 egg yolk

1 beaten egg, for glazing

2 tablespoons demerara sugar, for sprinkling

300 ml/1¼ cup double/heavy cream

50 g/⅓ cup icing/confectioners' sugar

1 teaspoon pure vanilla extract

strawberry jam/jelly (see page 11)

a baking sheet, lightly oiled

a large piping bag fitted with a large star-shaped nozzle/tip

makes 12

Sift the flour and salt into a large mixing bowl. Add the butter and rub it together with your fingertips, until it resembles fine breadcrumbs.

Heat the milk in a saucepan set over a gentle heat until warm, then stir in the sugar and yeast. Remove the milk from the heat and whisk in the egg and egg yolk.

Pour most of the liquid into the flour and mix to a soft, but not wet dough (you may not need all the liquid). Knead the dough for about 5 minutes or until the mixture is smooth and slightly springy.

Put the dough in an oiled bowl and roll to coat well. Cover with clingfilm/plastic wrap and leave in a warm place for about 1 hour, or until it has doubled in size.

Knock back the risen dough (see page 8) and knead for a minute or so. Roll the dough into a long sausage and cut it into 12 equal pieces. Take one piece of dough and make a cage out of one hand over it on the work surface and gently roll your hand in circles until you have made a smooth ball. Repeat with the remaining dough. Place the buns on the prepared baking sheet, with about 5 cm/2 in. between each one. Cover with a clean kitchen towel and leave in a warm place for about 30–45 minutes, or until they have nearly doubled in size.

Preheat the oven to 190°C (375°F) Gas 5.

Brush the tops of the buns with the beaten egg and sprinkle with the demerara sugar. Bake for 20–25 minutes or until golden brown. Transfer the buns to a wire rack to cool completely.

Whip the cream to stiff peaks. Whisk in the vanilla. Sift over the icing/confectioners' sugar and whisk again. Spoon the cream into the prepared piping bag. Make a deep slit in each bun, spread a layer of strawberry jam/jelly in each bun and pipe in a generous amount of cream. These are best served immediately.

Louise Cake

Louise cake hails from New Zealand and straddles somewhere between a slice and a cake. A rectangle of soft and cakey shortbread is topped with jam, before a final layer of billowing coconut meringue is spread on top. Louise cake makes the perfect portable snack for long journeys and lazy picnics in the sun.

75 g/5 tablespoons unsalted butter, softened

150 g/1 cup caster/ granulated sugar

2 large eggs, separated

150 g/1¼ cups plain/ all-purpose flour

1 teaspoon baking powder

seeds of 1 vanilla pod

1 tablespoon whole milk

5 tablespoons raspberry jam/jelly (see page 11)

a pinch of salt

50 g/½ cup desiccated/ shredded coconut, plus an extra 30–40 g/ ⅓ cup for sprinkling

a 25 x 20-cm/10 x 8-in. cake pan, greased and lined with baking parchment

makes 10

Preheat the oven to 180°C (350°F) Gas 4.

In a large mixing bowl, cream the butter and 50 g/¼ cup of the sugar together until light and fluffy before whisking in the egg yolks, one at a time. Sift over the flour and baking powder and mix together. Add the vanilla and milk and whisk until you have a fairly stiff cake batter. Spread the mixture in an even layer in the prepared cake pan, pressing it right into the corners.

Next, spread the jam/jelly over the base in an even layer – it is easier to spread the jam/jelly if you stir it to slacken it first.

In a spotlessly clean bowl, whisk the egg whites and salt together with clean beaters until stiff. Gradually whisk in the remaining sugar, a little at a time, until you are left with a smooth and glossy meringue.

Fold in 50 g/⅓ cup of desiccated/shredded coconut and spread the coconut meringue over the layer of jam/jelly. Sprinkle over the remaining coconut and bake for 25–30 minutes.

Leave the cake to cool for 10 minutes before slicing into 10 equal rectangles while still warm. Once completely cool, use an off-set palette knife to transfer the slices on to a serving plate.

Whoopie Pies

Whoopie pies are not, in fact, pies at all, rather they are somewhere between a cookie and a cake – like a mini cake sandwich. It is the official sweet treat of Maine, but Pennsylvania and New Hampshire both claim the whoopie pie as their own too. They are thought to have been introduced by Amish women and made from leftover cake batter. When the Amish men discovered them in their lunchboxes, apparently they would shout, 'Whoopie!'

For the cookies

75 g/3½ oz. dark/ bittersweet chocolate, broken into pieces
120 ml/½ cup whole milk
1 tablespoon very strong coffee
150 g/¾ cup dark muscovado sugar
60 g/5 tablespoons unsalted butter, softened
1 large egg, beaten
225 g/1¾ cups plain/ all-purpose flour
35 g/3 tablespoons cocoa
1 teaspoon bicarbonate of soda/baking soda
¼ teaspoon salt
icing/confectioners' sugar, to dust

For the filling

2 egg whites
65 g/⅓ cup caster/ granulated sugar
a pinch of cream of tartar
1 teaspoon pure vanilla extract

2 baking sheets, lined with baking parchment
a small ice cream scoop (optional)
a large piping bag fitted with a star-shaped nozzle/tip (optional)

makes 15

Preheat the oven to 180°C (350°F) Gas 4.

To make the cookies, put the chocolate, milk, coffee and 50 g/ ¼ cup of the sugar into a saucepan and set over a gentle heat. Stir until the chocolate has melted and the sugar has dissolved. Remove from the heat and leave to cool completely.

In a large mixing bowl, cream together the butter and remaining sugar until pale and fluffy. Gradually beat in the egg before whisking in the chocolate mixture. Sift the flour, cocoa and bicarbonate of soda/baking soda over the wet ingredients. Add the salt and fold in gently until thoroughly combined.

Use a small ice cream scoop (or cook'sl tablespoon) to drop 30 neat mounds of the mixture on to the prepared baking sheets, with a gap in between each one to allow for spreading. Bake for 8–10 minutes, or until an inserted cocktail stick/toothpick comes out clean. Transfer to a wire rack and leave to cool completely before filling.

To make the filling, whisk everything except the vanilla extract in a large heatproof bowl set over a pan of barely simmering water, until the sugar has dissolved and the whites are warm. Take the bowl off the heat and continue to whisk until stiff and glossy. This can take several minutes, so use an electric whisk and be patient. Whisk in the vanilla extract.

Spoon or pipe the filling on to a cookie and place another on top to sandwich. Repeat with the remaining cookies. Dust with icing/confectioners' sugar to serve.

Who can resist a cake that comes complete with its own wings? These sweet little fairy cakes can't fail to impress. I have updated these dainty classics with a fresh raspberry buttercream paired with a fluffy white chocolate sponge.

White Chocolate Butterfly Cakes
with raspberry buttercream

For the cakes

115 g/6 oz. white chocolate

1 tablespoon whole milk

2 large eggs, separated

a pinch of salt

115 g/8 tablespoons unsalted butter

115 g/²⁄₃ cup caster/ superfine sugar

1 teaspoon pure vanilla extract

145 g/1 cup plus 2 tablespoons self-raising/rising flour

¼ teaspoon baking powder

85 ml/⅓ cup sour cream

For the buttercream

50 g/½ cup fresh raspberries

100 g/6½ tablespoons unsalted butter, softened

200 g/1²⁄₃ cups icing/ confectioners' sugar

a 12-hole muffin pan, lined with paper cases

a large piping bag fitted with a star-shaped nozzle/tip

makes 12

Preheat the oven to 180°C (350°F) Gas 4.

Melt the chocolate with the milk in a heatproof bowl suspended over a bowl of barely simmering water. Leave to cool.

Whisk the egg whites and salt together in a large mixing bowl until they form soft peaks. Cream together the butter and caster/superfine sugar in another bowl, until pale and fluffy. Whisk in the egg yolks, one at a time, before adding the cooled melted chocolate and vanilla extract.

Sift over half of the flour and beat in, then add the sour cream and beat again to combine. Sift over the remaining flour and baking powder and mix again until thoroughly incorporated. Tip in the beaten egg whites and fold in with a large metal spoon, being careful not to beat the air out of the mixture.

Divide the cake batter among the paper cases and bake for 20–25 minutes, or until an inserted skewer comes out clean. Leave the cakes to cool.

Use a stick/immersion blender to blitz the raspberries into a purée and pass through a fine sieve/strainer to remove the seeds. In small bowl, whisk the butter until soft and creamy. Sift over half of the icing/ confectioners' sugar and whisk in half of the raspberry purée. Sift over the remaining icing/ confectioners' sugar and whisk in, before whisking in the remaining raspberry purée.

Cut the top off of each cold cake and cut in half to make 'wings'. Pipe a generous swirl of buttercream on top of each cake, before attaching the cake wings.

Lamingtons with passion fruit filling

For the cake
300 g/2½ sticks unsalted butter, softened
335 g/1⅔ cups caster/granulated sugar
6 eggs, beaten
600 g/4¾ cups self-raising/rising flour
2 teaspoons baking powder
335 ml/1⅓ cups whole milk
2 tablespoons pure vanilla extract
½ teaspoon salt

For the filling
200 g/¾ cup passion fruit pulp
150 g/1 stick plus 2 tablespoons unsalted butter, cut into cubes
2 whole eggs
2 egg yolks
175 g/¾ cup plus 2 tablespoons caster/granulated sugar
1 tablespoon cornflour/cornstarch

For the icing
300 g/10 oz. dark/bittersweet chocolate
300 ml/1¼ cups whole milk
100 g/¾ cup icing/confectioners' sugar, sifted
400 g/3½ cups desiccated/shredded coconut

a 25-cm/10-in. square cake pan, greased

makes 16

These classic Australian cakes are made from cubes of light, fluffy sponge cake dipped in chocolate icing and dunked in desiccated coconut. I have added a sunny twist with a central layer of sweet and tangy passion fruit curd.

Preheat the oven to 180°C (350°F) Gas 4.

To make the cake, cream the butter and sugar together in a large mixing bowl until light and fluffy, before gradually whisking in the eggs. Sift together the flour and baking powder into a small mixing bowl.

Whisk in one third of the flour mixture into the creamed mixture. Next, whisk in a third of the milk and continue to alternate between flour and milk until everything is fully combined. Whisk in the vanilla extract and salt and pour the batter into the prepared pan. Level the top with a palette knife and bake for 40 minutes–1 hour, or until an inserted skewer comes out clean.

Leave the cake to cool in the pan for 10 minutes before turning out to cool completely on a wire rack.

For the passion fruit curd, blitz the pulp in a food processor to help loosen the flesh from the seeds and pass it all through a fine sieve/strainer. Put the passion fruit juice and butter in a saucepan set over a gentle heat. Stir until the butter is melted.

Whisk the whole eggs, yolks, sugar and cornflour/cornstarch together in a large mixing bowl until pale and fluffy. Pour the hot passion fruit mixture into the egg mixture and whisk together, before pouring it all back into the saucepan. Continue to whisk gently for several minutes until the curd has thickened enough to coat the back of a spoon.

If you are not going to use the curd immediately, pour the hot mixture into a sterilized jar (see the tip on page 11) and, once cool, the curd can be left in the fridge for up to 10 days.

For the chocolate icing, melt the chocolate with the milk in a heatproof bowl over a pan of barely simmering water. Take off the heat and whisk in the sifted icing/confectioners' sugar.

To assemble, carefully trim off the darker edges of the cake and slice the cake horizontally in half. It may be easier to cool the cake in the fridge for 30 minutes beforehand to firm up. Spread one half of the cake liberally with the cold passion fruit curd and place the other half on top to sandwich the halves together.

Put the cake in the freezer for 20–30 minutes so it is firm enough to cut. Once chilled, slice the cake into 16 equal squares. Put the dessicated/shredded coconut on a plate. Put a cake square on a fork and dunk it into the chocolate icing then roll it in the coconut. Place on a clean sheet of baking parchment to set.

These sweet, buttery American swirls are fragrant with cinnamon and topped with a tangy cream cheese icing. Best eaten on the day they are baked, these rolls make the perfect weekend treat. You can put them in the fridge overnight for the second proving/rise and bake them for breakfast.

Cinnamon Rolls

For the dough

200 ml/³⁄₄ cup whole
    milk plus extra
    to glaze
550 g/4¹⁄₃ cups strong
    white bread flour
60 g/5 tablespoons cold
    butter, cut into cubes
60 g/5 tablespoons
    granulated sugar
1 teaspoon salt
7 g/0.25 oz. sachet fast-
    action/rapid-rise yeast
4 egg yolks
1 egg
sunflower oil, for oiling

For the filling

100 g/6¹⁄₂ tablespoons
    unsalted butter,
    melted
175 g/³⁄₄ cup plus 2
    tablespoons light
    muscovado sugar
1 tablespoon ground
    cinnamon
a pinch of salt

For the icing

75 g/¹⁄₃ cup full-fat
    cream cheese
3 tablespoons milk
2 teaspoons pure vanilla
    extract
150 g/1 generous cup
    icing/confectioners'
    sugar

a free-standing mixer
    with a dough hook
    (optional)
a 20 x 25-cm/8 x 10-in.
    ovenproof dish,
    greased

makes about 12

Put the milk in a saucepan set over a gentle heat to warm slightly. Meanwhile, sift the flour into a large mixing bowl and rub in the butter with your fingertips. Stir in the sugar, salt and yeast.

Make a well in the middle and pour in the milk and egg yolks and egg. Use a fork to beat the milk and eggs together and start bringing the dry ingredients into the wet until combined. It may take a little time for the flour to absorb all of the moisture, but keep mixing and it will happen.

Once the mixture is fully combined, tip it onto an oiled work surface and knead for about 10 minutes, or until the dough is smooth, soft and springy. The dough should be moist but not sticky. Alternatively, you can make the dough in a freestanding mixer with a dough hook.

Oil a large bowl and put the dough into it. Cover the top with clingfilm/plastic wrap and leave it to rise somewhere warm for about 1 hour, or until the dough has doubled in size.

Knock back the dough and turn it out on to a work surface to knead for another minute or so. Roll the dough into a large rectangle (dimensions), about ½ cm/³⁄₁₆ in. thick. Liberally paint the rectangle with melted butter, leaving a 2.5-cm/1-in. gap around the edges. Stir together the sugar, cinnamon and salt and sprinkle it evenly over the dough. Gently press the filling into the dough.

Beginning with the longest edge of the rectangle facing you, tightly roll the dough into a sausage. Pinch together the seam and roll the sausage over, seam-side down. Cut the dough into 12 equal pieces. Arrange the rolls next to each other, with a little gap in between each one, cut-side down, in the prepared dish. Cover the dish with a clean kitchen towel and leave somewhere warm to rise again for about 1 hour, or until almost double in size.

Preheat the oven to 190°C (375°F) Gas 5.

Brush with milk to glaze and bake for 20–25 minutes or until golden brown and well risen. While the rolls are baking, mix together the cream cheese icing ingredients until completely smooth. Remove the rolls from the oven and leave them to cool slightly before spreading them generously with icing.

These rolls are delicious served warm or cold.

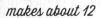

Rock Cakes

These tasty little cakes are so named because of their resemblance to rocks, not because they are rock hard! A traditional British teatime treat, rock cakes are child's play to make. In fact, they require such minimal labour, you can palm them off on your children to rustle up while you put your feet up.

220 g/1¾ cups self-raising/rising flour

1 teaspoon baking powder

75 g/⅓ cup caster/granulated sugar

a pinch of salt

110 g/7 tablespoons cold butter, cut into cubes

1 egg

1 tablespoon whole milk

50 g/⅓ cup dried (Zante) currants

50 g/⅓ cup sultanas/golden raisins

50 g/⅓ cup (dark) raisins

2 baking sheets, lined with baking parchment

makes 12

Preheat the oven to 180°C (350°F) Gas 4.

Sift the flour and baking powder into a large mixing bowl and stir in the sugar and salt. Rub the butter into the flour mixture with the tips of your fingers, until the mixture resembles fine breadcrumbs.

Make a well in the centre and crack in the egg and add the milk. Use a fork to whisk the egg and milk together and gradually mix the dry ingredients into the wet. Once combined, the mixture should be stiff but not dry. You can add a little extra milk at this stage if you need to. Add the remaining ingredients and mix well.

Dollop rounded teaspoons of mixture on to the prepared baking sheets, with a space in between to allow for spreading. Bake for 15–20 minutes, or until firm and slightly golden. Transfer the rock cakes to a wire rack to cool.

Fat Rascals

These mischievously named teacakes hail from Yorkshire and have been made famous by the legendary Betty's Tea Rooms in Harrogate. The 'fat' round cakes are decorated to make a cheeky face, hence the 'rascal'.

150 g/1¼ cups plain/
    all-purpose flour,
    plus extra for dusting
150 g/1¼ self-raising/
    rising flour
1 teaspoon baking
    powder
a pinch of salt
150 g/1 stick plus
    2 tablespoons cold
    unsalted butter,
    cut into cubes
75 g/⅓ cup caster/
    granulated sugar
50 g/⅓ cup dried
    (Zante) currants
50 g/⅓ cup sultanas/
    golden raisins
50 g/⅓ cup (dark)
    raisins

1 teaspoon ground
    cinnamon
½ teaspoon grated
    nutmeg
finely grated zest of
    1 orange and 1 lemon
50 ml/3 tablespoons
    whole milk
1 egg, beaten

To glaze and finish
1 egg, beaten
a splash of whole milk
50 g/½ cup flaked/
    slivered almonds
24 glacé cherries

*2 baking sheets, lined
   with baking parchment*

makes 12

Preheat the oven to 200°C (400°F) Gas 6 and put the baking sheets into the oven to heat.

In a large mixing bowl, sift together the flours, baking powder and salt. Rub the butter into the flour mixture with your fingertips, until the mixture resembles fine breadcrumbs. Stir in the sugar, dried fruit, spices and orange and lemon zest. Stir in the milk and egg until the mixture just forms a dough.

Tip the mixture onto a work surface lightly dusted with flour and cut into 6 pieces. Put on the baking sheet and form each piece gently into a mound, to create a 'fat' face. To glaze, combine the egg and milk and brush the top of each mound and decorate by making two glacé cherry eyes and a toothy grin made of flaked almonds. Bake for 15–20 minutes or until firm and golden. Serve the fat rascals warm.

Scones

It is believed that these sweet, quick breads originated in Scotland in the early 1500s, made with oats and cooked on a griddle, much like Scottish bannocks are today. Scones have evolved into light, fluffy rounds served with thick clotted cream and strawberry jam. Whether you insist on cream before jam or vice versa, and indeed whether you pronounce scone to rhyme with 'gone' or 'cone', a cream tea just wouldn't be the same without these delicious British bakes.

325 g/2½ cups plus
  1 tablespoon self-
  raising/rising flour,
  plus extra for dusting
1 teaspoon baking
  powder
a pinch of salt
75 g/5 tablespoons cold
  butter, cut into cubes
75 g/⅓ cup caster/
  granulated sugar

160 ml/⅔ cup whole
  milk
2 teaspoons lemon juice
1 egg, beaten

To serve
clotted (thick) cream
strawberry jam/jelly
  (see page 11)
a 5-cm/2-in. cookie
  cutter

makes 8–10

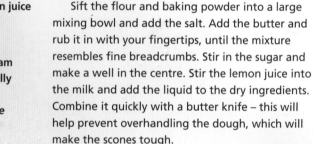

Preheat the oven to 220°C (425°F) Gas 7 and place the baking sheet in the oven to heat.

Sift the flour and baking powder into a large mixing bowl and add the salt. Add the butter and rub it in with your fingertips, until the mixture resembles fine breadcrumbs. Stir in the sugar and make a well in the centre. Stir the lemon juice into the milk and add the liquid to the dry ingredients. Combine it quickly with a butter knife – this will help prevent overhandling the dough, which will make the scones tough.

Dust a little flour onto the work surface and tip the dough out. Scatter a little extra flour over the dough and on your hands and lightly knead the dough. Roll or pat the dough down to make a 4-cm/1½-in. deep round.

Dip the cutter into some flour. Plunge into the dough – do not twist the cutter as this can affect the rise. Repeat until you can make no more and squidge the dough back together before patting down and cutting out some more. Brush the tops with a little beaten egg. Remove the hot baking sheet from the oven and carefully place the scones onto it. Bake for 10–12 minutes, or until well risen and golden on top.

Scones are best eaten on the day they are made, still warm and generously smothered with clotted cream and strawberry jam/jelly.

Chocolate & Hazelnut Brownies

The chocolate brownie is said to have been created at the Palmer House Kitchen Hotel in Chicago at the request of Bertha Palmer to be served at the Columbian Exposition World Fair in 1893. Despite only gaining popularity in the early 20th century, it feels like brownies have been part of American food culture forever. A sticky, dense square of chocolate cake, perfect for packed lunches, the brownie is enjoyed the world over.

250 g/8 oz. dark/
    bittersweet chocolate,
    broken into pieces
250 g/2 sticks unsalted
    butter
125 g/½ cup plus 2
    tablespoons light
    muscovado sugar
125 g/½ cup plus 2
    tablespoons caster/
    granulated sugar
4 eggs, beaten
¼ teaspoon salt
2 teaspoons pure vanilla
    extract
75 g/⅔ cup rice flour
50 g/⅓ cup plus 1
    tablespoon cocoa
    powder
½ teaspoon baking
    powder
½ teaspoon bicarbonate
    of soda/baking soda
100 g/3½ oz. whole
    milk chocolate/
    semisweet drops
75 g/½ cup chopped
    hazelnuts

a 20-cm/8-in. square
    cake pan, greased and
    lined with baking
    parchment

makes 16

Preheat the oven to 160°C (325°F) Gas 3.

Put the chocolate and butter in a heatproof bowl suspended over a pan of barely simmering water. Stir every now and then, until all the ingredients have melted.

In the meantime, whisk together the sugars, eggs and salt in a large bowl until light and creamy. Whisk in the chocolate mixture and vanilla extract.

Sift over the flour, cocoa, baking powder, bicarbonate of soda/baking soda and mix together. Fold in the chocolate chips and nuts and pour the mixture into the prepared cake pan. Level the top with a palette knife and bake for 35–40 minutes. An inserted skewer should still have a little stickiness left on it.

Leave to cool in the cake pan on a wire rack before turning out and cutting into 16 equal squares.

Chelsea Buns

These old-fashioned spiced fruit buns were created in the 1700s at The Bun House in Chelsea, London. Soft, sticky and deliciously tempting, these squidgy bakes hit all the right notes for a perfect, buttery afternoon tea.

450 g/3½ cups strong white flour, plus extra for dusting

1 teaspoon salt

7 g/0.25 oz. sachet fast-action/rapid-rise yeast

5 tablespoons caster/granulated sugar

300 ml/1¼ cups whole milk plus 2 tablespoons to glaze

40 g/2½ tablespoons unsalted butter, softened

1 egg, beaten

sunflower oil, for oiling

sugar glaze (see page 9)

For the filling

30 g/2 tablespoons unsalted butter, melted

75 g/⅓ cup dark muscovado sugar

3 teaspoons ground cinnamon

25 g/2½ tablespoons dried (Zante) currants

75 g/½ cup (dark) raisins

25 g/2½ tablespoons dried sour cherries or cranberries

25 g/2½ tablespoons sultanas/golden raisins

a large baking sheet, lightly oiled

makes 10

Sift the flour into a large mixing bowl and add the salt to one side and the yeast and 3 tablespoons of the sugar to the other. Put the 300 ml/1¼ cups milk and the butter in a saucepan over a gentle heat and stir until the butter has melted. The milk must not be hotter than lukewarm or it will kill the yeast, so you may have to leave it to cool for a few minutes.

Pour the warm milk mixture and the beaten egg into the flour and mix until everything starts coming together and forming a dough. Tip the dough out on a lightly floured surface and knead with the heel of your hands, until the dough is smooth and elastic. If the dough still feels sticky after 10 minutes add a little extra flour.

Lightly oil a large bowl, put the dough inside and cover with clingfilm/plastic wrap. Put the bowl in a warm place for about 1 hour, or until the dough has doubled in size.

Knock back the dough and turn out on to a lightly floured surface. Roll out the dough into a rectangle about ½ cm/³⁄₁₆ in. thick.

Brush all over with the melted butter, then sprinkle over the muscovado sugar, cinnamon and dried fruit. Carefully roll the dough up into a tight sausage shape and,

with the joining crease underneath, cut 10 equal pieces.

Lightly oil a baking sheet and arrange the buns, swirl-side up, with a small gap in between. Cover with a clean kitchen towel and leave to prove somewhere warm for about 30 minutes.

Preheat the oven to 200°C (400°F) Gas 6. Bake for 20–25 minutes, or until risen and golden-brown.

Meanwhile, to make a sugar glaze put the remaining 2 tablespoons sugar and 2 tablespoons milk together in a pan and stir over a gentle heat until the sugar has dissolved. Stop stirring and bring to the boil. Simmer for a few minutes until the glaze has reduced and thickened up.

Remove the buns from the oven and brush with the sugar glaze. Transfer to a wire rack to cool.

Large Cakes

Lemon Drizzle Cake

Who can resist this intensely lemony loaf cake? It has long been a favourite at teatime on British tables and for very good reason. The featherlight sponge is stabbed with a skewer while hot from the oven, before being soaked in lemon syrup. Be warned, it is incredibly hard to stop at a single slice.

For the cake

110 g/7 tablespoons unsalted butter, softened
175 g/¾ cup plus 2 tablespoons caster/granulated sugar
175 g/1⅓ cups self-raising/rising flour, sifted
1 teaspoon baking powder
a pinch of salt
2 large eggs
4 tablespoons whole milk
finely grated zest of 2 unwaxed lemons

For the topping

100 g/½ cup caster/granulated sugar
juice of 2 lemons

a 1 kg/2 lb loaf pan, lined with parchment paper

serves 8–10

Preheat the oven to 180°C (350°F) Gas 4.

Put all the cake ingredients, except the lemon zest, into a large mixing bowl and, using an electric hand whisk, thoroughly combine until the mixture is creamy and has a dropping consistency. Fold through the lemon zest and pour the cake batter out into the prepared loaf pan. Level the top with a palette knife and bake for 30–35 minutes, or until an inserted skewer comes out clean.

In the meantime, stir the lemon juice and sugar together in a jug/pitcher to make the drizzle topping. Once the cake has baked, remove it from the oven and stab it all over with a skewer to create lots of fine holes for the syrup to soak through. Pour the lemon syrup over the hot cake and leave the cake to cool completely in its pan on top of a wire rack, before turning out.

Hummingbird Cake

This moist cake hails from the American South. The cake includes tropical banana and pineapple, is lightly spiced with cinnamon and has a nutty pecan crunch, topped with tangy cream cheese frosting.

For the cake

3 eggs

175 g/$\frac{3}{4}$ cup plus 2 tablespoons caster/granulated sugar

250 ml/1 cup sunflower oil

2 ripe bananas, mashed

100 g/$\frac{2}{3}$ cup pecan nuts, broken into pieces

250 g/1 generous cup finely chopped fresh or canned pineapple, drained, 2 tablespoons of juice reserved

325 g/2$\frac{1}{2}$ cups plus 1 tablespoon plain/all-purpose flour

2 teaspoons ground cinnamon

$\frac{1}{2}$ teaspoon freshly grated nutmeg

1$\frac{1}{2}$ teaspoons bicarbonate of soda/baking soda

1 teaspoon salt

1 quantity cream cheese frosting (see page 9)

50 g/$\frac{1}{3}$ cup pecan nuts, for decoration (optional)

2 x 20-cm/8-in. sandwich pans/shallow round cake pans, greased and lined with baking parchment

serves 8–10

Preheat to oven to 180°C (350°F) Gas 4.

In a large mixing bowl, whisk the eggs and sugar until light and mousse-like. This can take several minutes, so I'd advise using an electric hand mixer to save your arms here. Whisk in the oil until smooth. Mix in the banana, pecans, pineapple and pineapple juice.

Sift over the flour and add the spices, bicarbonate of soda/baking soda and salt. Fold the dry ingredients into the wet with a large metal spoon.

Divide the batter between the prepared cake pans and bake for 45–50 minutes, or until an inserted skewer comes out clean. Leave the cakes to cool in their pans on a wire rack for 10 minutes, before turning the cakes out onto the rack to cool completely.

In the meantime, make the frosting following the instructions on page 9.

Place one cake on a serving plate and spread half of the cream cheese frosting over the cake. Place the second cake on top and use a palette knife to spread the top and sides of the cake with the remaining frosting. Decorate the sides or top of the cake with pecans, if you like.

Angel Cake

Not to be confused with the American classic Angel Food Cake, this three-layer confection illustrates British baking whimsy at its best. Angel cake was always a favourite of mine as a child, in part thanks to its attractive shades of powder pink, lemon yellow and chalk white, but also because of its featherlight fatless sponge, which is so pleasingly fluffy that stopping at one slice is a nigh on impossible feat.

For the cake
6 egg whites
a pinch of salt
1 teaspoon cream of tartar
175 g/³⁄₄ cup plus 2 tablespoons caster/granulated sugar
2 teaspoons pure vanilla extract
100 g/³⁄₄ cup plain/all-purpose flour
a few drops of yellow and pink food dye

For the buttercream
50 g/3 tablespoons unsalted butter, softened
75 g/½ cup icing/confectioners' sugar
2 teaspoons pure vanilla extract

a 20 x 25-cm/8 x 10-in. cake pan, greased and lined with baking parchment

serves 10–12

Preheat oven to 180°C (350°F) Gas 4.

Take a piece of foil approximately 1.25 m/50 in. long and fold it in half to double up its strength. Next, trim it widthways so it is 20 cm/8 in. wide and will snugly fit inside the cake pan. Starting from the left, measure just over 7 cm/3 in. and make a fold in the foil. Next, using the fold you have made as a size guide, create a pleat. This is to separate the different-coloured cake batters. Repeat this process so that you are left with three compartments. Grease the foil and sit it inside the prepared pan.

To make the cake, whisk the egg whites, salt and cream of tartar together in a large mixing bowl until frothy. Add the sugar and whisk on high speed until the mixture becomes stiff and glossy. Whisk in the pure vanilla extract and sift the flour over the top of the mixture. Fold the flour in with a large metal spoon.

Put one-third of the mixture in the first compartment in the prepared pan and level the top with a palette knife. Divide the remaining batter into two bowls and dye one half yellow and the other pink. Spoon the yellow mixture into one of the remaining compartments and the pink into the other. Level their tops with a palette knife (give it a quick rinse in between to keep the colours pure).

Bake for 15 minutes or until the top is slightly golden and the cakes have started to shrink away from the sides of the cake pan.

Put the cake pan on top of a wire rack to cool for 10 minutes before turning the cakes out on to the rack to cool completely.

In the meantime, make the buttercream filling. In a bowl, whisk the butter until very soft and sift over the icing/confectioners' sugar. Whisk to combine. Add the vanilla and whisk again until you have a smooth and fluffy buttercream.

Place the yellow cake on a serving plate and spread the top with half of the buttercream. Position the pink cake on top. Spread the remaining buttercream on top of the pink cake and top it with the white cake before serving.

Victoria Sponge

Perhaps the most well loved and famous British cake, the Victoria sponge, or Victoria sandwich as it is sometimes known, was named after Queen Victoria, who was partial to a slice with her afternoon tea. Anna, the Duchess of Bedford, is credited with creating the recipe while she was a lady in waiting for the Queen in the latter half of the 1800s.

220 g/1 cup plus 2 tablespoons caster/granulated sugar

220 g/15 tablespoons unsalted butter, softened

4 duck eggs (or you can use 5 large/jumbo hen's), beaten

1 tablespoon pure vanilla extract (optional)

220 g/1½ cups self-raising/rising flour

1 teaspoon baking powder

a pinch of salt

a splash of whole milk, if needed

3–4 tablespoons raspberry jam/jelly (see page 11)

icing/confectioners' sugar, for dusting

2 x 20-cm/8-in. sandwich pans/round shallow cake pans, greased and lined with baking parchment

serves 8–10

Preheat the oven to 180 °C (350°F) Gas 4.

In a large mixing bowl, cream the butter and sugar together until light and fluffy. Gradually beat in the eggs, a little at a time to prevent the mixture curdling. Stir in the pure vanilla extract, if using. Sift over the flour and baking powder and add the salt. Fold the dry ingredients into the wet until thoroughly combined. The mixture should be light and fluffy and of a good dropping consistency; add a little milk if the mixture is too stiff.

Divide the mixture between the prepared cake pans and level their tops with a palette knife. Bake for 20–25 minutes, or until an inserted skewer comes out clean.

Leave the cakes to cool in their pans for 10 minutes before turning out on to a wire rack. To prevent the cake tops having wire rack marks, place a clean kitchen towel over one hand and upturn the cake on to your flat palm before transferring it, base-side down, to the wire rack to cool.

Once completely cool, place one cake on a serving plate, spread the top with the jam/jelly and place the other cake on top. Dust the top liberally with icing/confectioners' sugar to serve.

Black Forest Gâteau

I'm not sure I can think of a more tempting combination than cherry and chocolate. A ubiquitous staple of British dinner parties in the 1970s, the Black Forest Gâteau sadly fell out of favour. Now is the time to bring it back! Decadent, towering and boozy, this cake makes a stunning centrepiece to any celebration, no matter the occasion or the decade.

9 eggs, separated
a pinch of salt
250 g/1¼ cups caster/granulated sugar
250 g/8 oz. dark chocolate, melted and cooled
50 g/⅓ cup unsweetened cocoa
600 ml/2½ cups double/heavy cream
1 tablespoon icing/confectioners' sugar, sifted
2 tablespoons Kirsch
500 g/1 lb. Kirsch-soaked cherries, drained (drained weight)
fresh cherries, to decorate (optional)
100 g/3½ oz. dark/bittersweet chocolate, grated, to decorate (optional)

3 x 20-cm/8-in. shallow, loose-bottomed cake pans, greased and lined with baking parchment

serves 8–10

Preheat the oven to 180°C (350°F) Gas 4.

Put the egg whites and salt in a large mixing bowl and whisk to stiff peaks. Set aside until later. In a separate bowl, whisk the egg yolks and sugar together until pale and mousse-like and the mixture leaves a ribbon trail when you lift the beaters.

Whisk in the cooled melted chocolate before beating in one-third of the stiff egg whites. Fold the remaining egg whites into the chocolate mixture with a large metal spoon, until fully combined. Sift over the cocoa and fold through carefully until there are no remaining streaks in the batter. Be careful not to knock the air out of the mixture.

Divide the mixture among the prepared pans and bake for 20 minutes or until an inserted skewer comes out clean. Leave the cakes to cool in their pans for 10 minutes before turning out on wire racks to cool completely.

When the cakes are cold, whip the cream in a bowl until stiff before whisking in the icing/confectioners' sugar and Kirsch. Place one of the cakes on a serving plate. Use a palette knife to spread a generous layer of cream over the top and scatter with half the Kirsch-soaked cherries. Add a second layer of cake and spread over more cream and the remaining Kirsch-soaked cherries. Top with the final layer of cake and spread the remaining cream over the top and sides of the cake.

If you wish, you can pipe a few swirls of cream in a ring around the top of the cake for an extra flourish. Decorate the sides of the cake with grated chocolate and top with fresh cherries, if you like.

Top tip If you would prefer to make this cake alcohol free, substitute the cherries in Kirsch with stoned/pitted cherries in syrup and leave the Kirsch out of the whipped cream filling.

Passion Cake

This deliciously moist carrot cake has the fragrant additions of banana and coconut. Apparently, the cake was created for weddings as a cheaper alternative to traditional fruitcake. It was named passion cake in celebration of the love and union of marriage. It doesn't actually contain any passion fruit, but I sometimes like to scoop out some passion fruit pulp to decorate the top.

For the cake

4 large eggs
300 ml/1¼ cups sunflower oil
400 g/2 cups light muscovado sugar
450 g/3 cups grated carrot
zest of ½ orange
1 large ripe banana, mashed
100 g/⅔ cup roughly chopped walnuts
50 g/½ cup desiccated coconut
350 g/2¾ cups self-raising/rising flour
2 teaspoons bicarbonate of soda/baking soda
1 tablespoon ground cinnamon
½ teaspoon grated nutmeg
1 teaspoon ground ginger
½ teaspoon salt
1 quantity cream cheese frosting (see page 9)

To decorate

200 g/1⅓ cups coarsely chopped walnuts
pulp of 1–2 ripe passion fruit

2 x 23-cm/9-in. sandwich pans/round shallow cake pans, greased and lined with baking parchment

serves 10–12

Preheat the oven to 150°C (300°F) Gas 2.

In a large mixing bowl, whisk together the eggs, oil and sugar until fully combined and slightly frothy. Add the carrot, orange zest, banana, walnuts and coconut and mix together. Sift over the flour, bicarbonate of soda/baking soda and spices and fold in with the salt.

Divide the batter between the prepared pans and bake for 35–45 minutes, or until an inserted skewer comes out clean.

Leave the cakes to cool completely in their pans on top of a wire rack for 10 minutes, before turning out onto the rack to cool completely.

In the meantime, make the cream cheese frosting following the instructions on page 9. Whisk in a little lemon juice if desired.

Place one of the cakes on a serving plate and spread the top with half the frosting. Position the second cake on top and spread the remaining frosting over the top and sides of the cake. Gently press the chopped walnuts to the sides of the cake, if using, and decorate with passion fruit pulp on the top as an ode to the cake's name, if you wish.

Opera Cake

For the Joconde
7 eggs (see method)
**175 g/1¼ cups icing/
confectioners' sugar,
sifted**
**175 g/1¼ cups ground
almonds**
**40 g/3 tablespoons
butter, melted**
**50 g/¼ cup plus 1
tablespoon plain/all-
purpose flour, sifted**
a pinch of salt
**50 g/¼ cup
caster/superfine sugar**

For the base
**50 g/1½ oz. dark/
bittersweet chocolate,
tempered (see page 8)**

For the syrup
200 ml/¾ cup coffee
**1 tablespoon caster/
granulated sugar**

For the buttercream
**200 g/1 cup caster/
granulated sugar**
**200 g/1¾ sticks
unsalted butter**
2 tablespoons coffee

For the ganache
**250 g/8 oz. dark/
bittersweet chocolate**
**250 ml/1 cup single/light
cream**
**2 tablespoons unsalted
butter, softened**
gold leaf, to decorate

*2 x 38 x 25-cm/15 x 10-
in. roulade/jelly roll
pans, lined with
baking parchment*

serves 12–15

Preheat the oven to 180°C (350°F) Gas 4.

Read the recipe method then separate and prepare the eggs as necessary for each element before you start. Set them aside ready.

To make the *Joconde*, whisk 2 whole eggs, 2 egg yolks and the icing/confectioners' sugar together in a large mixing bowl. Add the ground almonds and continue whisking on high speed for about 5 minutes. Stir in the butter and flour until thoroughly incorporated. In a separate bowl, whisk 5 egg whites and the salt until softly peaking. Whisk in the sugar in two stages and continue whisking until the mixture is stiff and glossy. Add one-third of the egg white mixture to the almond mixture and stir vigorously to slacken the batter. Fold in the remaining egg white mixture and pour into the prepared pans. Use a palette knife to smooth the mixture out.

Bake in the oven for 8–12 minutes, or until the *Joconde* is no longer sticky to touch. Remove from the oven and leave to cool in its pan for about 10 minutes before turning out onto a wire rack to cool completely.

To make the coffee syrup, dissolve the sugar in the espresso coffee in a glass measuring jug/cup and set aside.

To make the coffee buttercream, put the sugar and 2 tablespoons water in a pan and place over a gentle heat until the sugar has dissolved. Increase the heat slightly and simmer until it reaches the soft ball stage – this happens at around 120°C (250°F). Whisk 3 egg yolks in a bowl. Trickle the hot syrup into the eggs, whisking all the time. Once the

mixture is pale and fluffy, leave it to cool a little before whisking in the butter and espresso coffee.

To make the chocolate ganache, break up the chocolate and put it in a heatproof bowl. Scald (see page 8) the cream in a saucepan or pot and pour it over the chocolate. Leave to stand for 1 minute before mixing it in with a rubber spatula. Whisk in the butter and leave to cool slightly.

To assemble the cakes, trim both the sheets of *Joconde* into equal-size rectangles and cut each rectangle in half so that you have 4 equal-size pieces of cake.

To make the crisp chocolate base, turn one piece of *Joconde* over and paint it with the tempered chocolate. Leave to set at room temperature before turning it over on to a sheet of baking parchment resting on a large chopping board. Use a pastry brush to apply a liberal amount of the coffee syrup.

Evenly spread a layer of coffee buttercream about 5-mm/¾-in. thick over the coffee-soaked sponge. Place another layer of *Joconde* on top and soak with syrup as before. Spread a thin, even layer of ganache over the top. Leave to set at room temperature.

Top with a third layer of coffee-soaked *Joconde* and buttercream before placing the final layer of coffee-soaked *Joconde* on top. Top with more ganache then leave to set at room temperature.

Once set, dip a long, sharp knife in hot water. Wipe it dry and trim each edge neatly. Decorate with gold leaf for a little extra glamour.

This opulent cake was created in France in the early 1900s and is named after the Paris Opera. The cake is also sometimes known as Gâteau Clichy, after Louis Clichy, the baker who invented it. This indulgent French dessert cake is the perfect celebration fare. It is made with layers of almond sponge cake, called *Joconde* in French, and is usually served cut in cubes.

Kugelhopf (Bundt Cake)

This sweet yeast cake is studded with dried fruit and nuts and baked in a bundt pan. The kugelhopf dates from the late 19th century and, although almost certainly originating from Austria, it is also a popular classic in Germany, Switzerland and Alsace.

280 ml/1 cup plus 3 tablespoons whole milk
110 g/7 tablespoons unsalted butter
100 g/½ cup caster/granulated sugar
2 tablespoons Kirsch or cherry brandy
7 g/0.25 oz. sachet fast-action/rapid-rise yeast
475 g/3¾ cups strong white flour
1 teaspoon salt
zest of 1 orange and 1 lemon
80 g/½ cup sultanas/golden raisins
80 g/½ cup (dark) raisins
80 g/½ cup sour/tart cherries
40 g/¼ cup mixed candied peel
50 g/½ cup flaked/slivered almonds
2 eggs, lightly beaten
about 20 whole blanched almonds
icing/confectioners' sugar, to dust
sunflower oil, for oiling (optional)

a free-standing mixer with a dough hook (optional)
a dough scraper (optional)
a 24-cm/9½-in. bundt pan, greased

serves 8–10

Heat the milk and butter in a saucepan set over a gentle heat until warm. Take off the heat and make sure it's not too hot (you should be able to dip your finger in it comfortably), or you will kill the yeast. Stir in the sugar, Kirsch and yeast. Set aside.

The next stage is easiest done in a free-standing mixer with a dough hook, but if you don't have one, it is perfectly possible to do by hand. Just prepare to get messy and make sure you have a dough scraper on hand.

Sift the flour and salt into a large mixing bowl. Stir in the zest, fruit and flaked/slivered almonds. Make a well in the middle and add the milk mixture and the eggs. At this stage, if using the machine, simply turn it on for 5–10 minutes and wait for the dough to leave the sides of the bowl clean. It is a very sticky dough, so don't expect it to look like your average bread dough.

If doing by hand, fork together the ingredients, before tipping it on to an oiled work surface. Oil your hands and pull the dough up and rotate it away from you before slapping it back down on the work surface. Continue this circular motion energetically, until the mixture starts to come together to form a very soft, elastic dough. It will be very sticky. Scrape it off the work surface (and your hands) every now and then with the dough scraper.

Place the whole blanched almonds, if using, into the depressions in the prepared pan and spoon the dough evenly on top. Cover the top with oiled clingfilm/plastic wrap. Put a kitchen towel over the top and leave somewhere warm for 1–2 hours, or until it has almost filled the pan.

Preheat the oven to 200°C (400°F) Gas 6.

Bake for 15 minutes. Cover loosely with foil and continue to bake for a further 20–25 minutes, or until an inserted skewer comes out clean. Leave to cool in its pan for 10 minutes on top of a wire rack, before turning out on to the wire rack to cool completely.

Once cold, transfer to a serving plate and dust with icing/confectioners' sugar. This is best eaten on the day it is made.

Very Vanilla Chiffon Cake

This American cake, invented in the 1920s, is incredibly light, moist and fluffy. I adore vanilla and the use of both vanilla pods and extract make this cake enticingly aromatic. The cakes looks beautiful when baked in a cake ring and filled with seasonal berries.

6 large eggs, separated
½ teaspoon salt
220 g plus 1 tablespoon/1¼ cups caster/superfine sugar
1 teaspoon white wine vinegar
130 ml/½ cup sunflower oil
seeds of 1 vanilla pod
2 tablespoons plus 1 teaspoon pure vanilla extract
220 g/1¾ cups plain/all-purpose flour
½ teaspoon bicarbonate of soda/baking soda
100 g/⅔ cup icing/confectioners' sugar, sifted
fresh blueberries and blackberries, to serve (optional)

a 25-cm/10-in. cake ring, greased and floured

serves 8–10

Preheat the oven to 180°C (350°F) Gas 4.

In a large mixing bowl, whisk the egg whites and salt to soft peaks. Add the 1 tablespoon of caster/superfine sugar and whisk to stiff peaks, then whisk in the vinegar and set aside.

Whisk the egg yolks, remaining caster/superfine sugar, oil, vanilla seeds and 2 tablespoons pure vanilla extract in a large bowl with an electric hand whisk for a few minutes. Sift the flour and bicarbonate of soda/baking soda over the wet ingredients and mix in.

Fold the egg whites into the batter with a large metal spoon and pour the mixture into the prepared pan. Bake for 35–40 minutes or until an inserted skewer comes out clean.

Leave to cool in its pan completely on a wire rack before turning out. Mix the remaining pure vanilla extract, the icing/confectioners' sugar and 1 tablespoon water in a small bowl to make a loose vanilla-flavoured icing. Fill the hole in the centre of the cake with the berries (if using) and drizzle the icing over the top of the cake.

Created in 1856 in Boston's Parker House Hotel, the Boston cream pie became the official dessert of Massachusetts in 1996. Despite its name, the Boston cream pie is not a pie at all, but a cake. Light vanilla sponge filled generously with *crème pâtissière* and topped with a dark chocolate glaze, Boston cream pie is so good it even has its own National Boston Cream Pie Day, celebrated on the 23rd of October every year.

Boston Cream Pie

For the cake
165 ml/²⁄₃ cup whole
    milk
25 g/2 tablespoons
    unsalted butter
2 eggs
2 egg yolks
175 g/³⁄₄ cup plus 2
    tablespoons caster/
    granulated sugar
1 tablespoon pure
    vanilla extract
250 g/2 cups plain/
    all-purpose flour
1 teaspoon baking
    powder
½ teaspoon salt

For the crème pâtissière
500 ml/2 cups whole milk
2 vanilla pods or
    1 tablespoon pure
    vanilla extract
2 eggs
4 egg yolks
75 g/¹⁄₃ cup caster/
    granulated sugar
50 g/¹⁄₃ cup cornflour/
    cornstarch, sifted
25 g/2 tablespoons
    unsalted butter,
    cut into small cubes

For the topping
100 ml/scant ½ cup
    single/light cream
100 g/3½ oz. dark/
    bittersweet chocolate,
    chopped

*a 20-cm/8-in. round cake
    pan, greased and
    lined with baking
    parchment*

Preheat the oven to 180°C (350°F) Gas 4.

To make the cake, put the milk and butter in a saucepan set over a gentle heat. You want the butter to melt, but you don't want the milk to boil, so keep an eye on it.

In the meantime, whisk the eggs, egg yolks and sugar together in a large bowl until pale and mousse-like. Gradually add the warm butter and milk, whisking on low speed all the time. Mix in the vanilla and sift the flour and baking powder over the top. Add the salt and fold the dry ingredients into the wet until fully incorporated.

Pour the batter into the prepared cake pan, level the top with a palette knife and bake for 35–45 minutes, or until an inserted skewer comes out clean. Leave the cake to cool in its pan for 10 minutes, before turning out on to a wire rack to cool completely.

To make the *crème pâtissière*, split the vanilla pods and scrape out the seeds. Put the milk and vanilla seeds and pods in a saucepan and simmer gently for 5 minutes.

In the meantime, put the eggs, egg yolks, sugar and cornflour/cornstarch in a heatproof bowl and whisk together until pale and creamy. Pour the hot milk over the egg mixture (strained if using vanilla pods and discard the pods) and whisk together before transferring the mixture back to the pan. Stir continuously over a gentle heat for 1–2 minutes, before increasing the heat and bringing to the boil. Keep stirring the bubbling mixture until the *crème pâtissiére* has thickened.

Take the pan off the heat and vigorously whisk in the butter until it has melted. Transfer to a jug/pitcher and cover in clingfilm/plastic wrap to prevent a skin forming. Once cool, transfer to the fridge. This can be made 2 or 3 days before needed.

To make the chocolate ganache topping, pour the cream into a saucepan and set over a low heat. Put the chopped chocolate in a heatproof bowl. Once the cream scalds (you don't need to bring it to the boil), pour it over the chocolate and leave to stand for 1 minute. Stir the chocolate and cream together until all the chocolate has melted and you are left with a thick and glossy ganache. Leave to cool slightly.

If the cake top has domed, use a long serrated knife to even it out, before cutting the cake horizontally in half. Place one half on a serving plate (if the cake did dome, it may be more attractive to use the bottom of the cake as the top). Spread the cold *crème pâtissiére* very thickly on the top (you might need to give it an extra whisk first). It will look like there is too much, but trust me on this one! Top the *crème pâtissiére* with the remaining cake half.

Pour the slightly cooled chocolate ganache over the top of the cake. Use a palette knife to encourage it to spread to the edges if necessary and let the chocolate drip down the sides of cake a little.

Leave the cake topping to set for at least 20 minutes before serving.

Mustikkapiirakka *(Finnish Blueberry Pie)*

150 g/1 stick plus
    2 tablespoons butter,
    softened
225 g/1 cup plus
    2 tablespoons caster/
    granulated sugar
2 eggs
seeds of 1 vanilla pod
200 g/1²⁄₃ cups rice flour
1 teaspoon baking
    powder
400 g/14 oz. fresh
    blueberries
250 ml/1 cup sour cream
50 ml/3 tablespoons
    buttermilk
1 tablespoon pure
    vanilla extract

*a 25-cm/10-in. loose-
    bottomed tart pan,
    greased*

serves 8–10

I first ate this delicious pie at a reindeer farm in the little village of Inari in northern Finland. Sweet, buttery and tangy, the mustikkapiirakka was so delicious, I was determined to recreate it as soon as I got home to London. Although it's called a pie, it's actually more of a cake.

Preheat the oven to 200°C (400°F) Gas 6.

Cream together the butter and 150 g/¾ cup of the sugar in a large mixing bowl until pale and fluffy. Beat in 1 egg and the vanilla seeds, before sifting over and folding in the flour and baking powder. You should be left with a fairly stiff batter. Spread the batter over the bottom and up the sides of the prepared pan and scatter the blueberries over the top.

Whisk together the sour cream, buttermilk, remaining sugar, egg and the pure vanilla extract and pour the mixture over the blueberries. Bake for 30 minutes then turn the oven down to 160°C (325°F) Gas 3 and bake for a further 30 minutes.

Turn off the oven and leave the pie inside the cooling oven for a further 10 minutes. Put the pan on a wire rack to cool completely, then remove the pie from the pan to serve.

Peanut Butter & Jelly Cake

The PB&J is an American classic for a reason. Salty, smooth peanut butter cut through with fruity seedless jam or jelly, this combination is irresistible. In cake form, this sponge is hard to beat.

300 g/1½ cups caster/
  granulated sugar
300 g/2½ sticks unsalted
  butter, softened
100 g/⅓ cup plus 1
  tablespoon smooth
  peanut butter
6 large eggs
300 g/2⅓ cups self-raising/
  rising flour, sifted
2 teaspoons baking
  powder
1 teaspoon salt
1 tablespoon pure vanilla
  extract
a splash of whole milk,
  if needed
6 tablespoons seedless
  grape or raspberry
  jam/jelly (see page 11)

For the buttercream
50 g/3 tablespoons
  unsalted butter,
  softened
50 g/3 tablespoons
  smooth peanut butter
200 g/1½ cups icing/
  confectioners' sugar
2 teaspoons pure vanilla
  extract
a splash of whole milk,
  if needed

*3 x 20-cm/8-in. round cake
  pans, greased and lined
  with baking parchment*

serves 10–12

Preheat the oven to 180°C (350°F) Gas 4.

To make the cake, put all of the ingredients, except for the milk and jam/jelly, in a large mixing bowl and whisk together with an electric hand mixer until completely combined, soft and fluffy. If the batter is too stiff, whisk in a splash of milk to slacken it slightly.

Divide the mixture evenly among the prepared cake pans, smooth over the tops with a palette knife and bake for 20–25 minutes, or until an inserted skewer comes out clean. Leave the cakes to cool in their pans, on a wire rack, for 10 minutes, before turning out on to the wire rack to cool completely.

In the meantime, make the buttercream. Whisk together the butter and peanut butter until fluffy. Sift over half of the icing/confectioners' sugar and whisk until fully combined. Sift over the remaining half of the icing/confectioners' sugar and whisk again for a couple of minutes. Whisk in the vanilla and then whisk in some milk to slacken the mixture, if necessary.

Place one cake on a serving plate and spread half of the jelly over the top. Place a second cake on top, before spreading the remaining jelly over the top. Place the final cake on top of the jelly. Spread one-third of the buttercream evenly over the top and sides of the cake, then chill for 30 minutes. Remove from the fridge and evenly spread the remaining buttercream on the top and sides of the cake.

Dorset Apple Cake

This rustic cake is moist, homely and irresistible. There are as many recipes for Dorset apple cake as there are Dorset bakers, but I have been reliably informed that apple cakes with 'Dorset' in the title must never include spice. Leave your cinnamon and nutmeg in the spice rack for another time. My version has a crunchy topping of demerara sugar and a subtle zing of lemon to complement the apples.

400 g/14 oz. apples (Bramleys, or something similarly crisp, sharp and sweet)

zest and juice of 1 unwaxed lemon

250 g/2 sticks unsalted butter, softened

250 g/1¼ cups light muscovado sugar

4 eggs

50 g/⅓ cup ground almonds

a pinch of salt

250 g/2 cups self-raising/rising flour

2 teaspoons baking powder

1 tablespoon demerara sugar

a 23-cm/9-in. round cake pan, greased and lined with baking parchment

serves 10–12

Preheat the oven to 180°C (350°F) Gas 4.

Core and chop the apples into roughly 1-cm/½-in. pieces and toss them in the lemon juice to prevent browning.

Cream the butter and sugar together in a large mixing bowl until pale and fluffy. Beat the eggs and gradually add them to the sugar and butter mixture, whisking thoroughly between each addition. If the mixture starts to curdle you can add a tablespoon of the flour. Whisk in the ground almonds and salt. Sift over the flour and baking powder before folding it into the mixture until fully combined.

Drain the apple pieces and add them to the batter, along with the lemon zest and fold through until the apple is evenly distributed. Pour into the prepared pan, smooth over the

top with a palette knife and scatter over an even layer of demerara sugar.

Bake for 1–1¼ hours, or until an inserted skewer comes out clean. Leave the cake to cool completely in its pan on top of a wire rack before turning out.

My devilishly hot twist on this American classic is rich with cocoa and studded with finely chopped fresh red chillies/chiles. You can, if you wish, reduce the heat on this cake and leave them out. Revert to tradition and simply add 2 teaspoons espresso coffee powder dissolved in 1 tablespoon of hot water to the mixture and forego the pleasingly silly chilli devil horns.

Devil's Food Cake

For the devil horns
2 long red fresh
   chillies/chiles
200 g/1 cup caster/
   granulated sugar

For the cake
250 g/2 sticks butter
250 ml/1 cup whole milk
125 g/^{2}/$_3$ cup dark
   muscovado sugar
175 g/^{3}/$_4$ cup plus
   2 tablespoons caster/
   granulated sugar
3 eggs
150 g/1 cup plus
   2 tablespoons plain/
   all-purpose flour
125 g/1 cup
   unsweetened cocoa
1 teaspoon bicarbonate
   of soda/baking soda
½ teaspoon baking
   powder
¼ teaspoon salt
4 fresh red chillies/
   chiles, deseeded
   and finely chopped

For the frosting
1 quantity cream cheese
   frosting (see page 9)
   omit the lemon zest
2–3 tablespoons of the
   chilli/chile syrup or
   2 teaspoons coffee
   powder dissolved in
   1 tablespoon hot water

*2 x 20-cm/ 8-in. cake
pans, greased and
lined with baking
parchment*

serves 12–15

First, make the chilli/chile horns, if using. Put the sugar and 200 ml/¾ cup water in a saucepan set over a gentle heat and stir until the sugar has fully dissolved. Increase the heat and boil for 1 minute. Meanwhile, prick the stalk end of the chillies with a needle or skewer. Reduce the heat, add the chillies and simmer gently for 40 minutes, or until they have begun to turn translucent and the sugar has slightly thickened. Turn off the heat and leave the chillies to cool in their syrup overnight.

Preheat the oven to 180°C (350°F) Gas 4.

Put the butter, milk and dark muscovado sugar in a saucepan and stir over a gentle heat until the sugar and butter have melted. Whisk together the caster/granulated sugar and eggs in a large mixing bowl until light and fluffy. Continue to whisk, while gradually adding the hot butter mixture. Sift over the

flour, cocoa, bicarbonate of soda/baking soda, baking powder and salt and whisk until fully combined.

Fold in the chopped chillies/chiles and divide the batter between the two prepared pans and bake for 25–30 minutes or until an inserted skewer comes out clean. Leave the cakes to cool in their pans on a wire rack for 10 minutes before turning out on to the wire rack to cool completely.

To make the frosting, follow the instructions on page 9 leaving out the lemon zest. Add the chilli/chile syrup and continue to whisk until soft and spreadable. Sandwich the cakes together with half the frosting and use a palette knife to spread the remaining icing over the top and sides of the cake, swirling the frosting to create a textured effect. Finally, place the two chilli/chile horns on either side of the top of the cake to make the cake extra devilish, if you wish.

Summer Berry Pavlova
with Elderflower Cream

Created in honour of the ballet dancer Anna Pavlova in the 1920s, this dessert has long been a bone of contention between Australians and New Zealanders. Whichever country is responsible for inventing this glorious meringue dessert, it has become a national dish of both. A crunchy exterior reveals a chewy marshmallowy centre. Piled with cream and fruit, a Pavlova is a perennial classic for very good reason.

6 egg whites
a pinch of salt
335 g/1²/₃ cups caster/granulated sugar
2 teaspoons cornflour/cornstarch
1 teaspoon white wine vinegar
seeds of 1 vanilla pod
700 g/1¾ lbs. mixed fresh summer berries
fresh mint sprigs, to decorate (optional)
icing/confectioners' sugar, to dust

For the elderflower cream
600 ml/2½ cups double/heavy cream
3–4 tablespoons elderflower cordial

a large baking sheet, lined with baking parchment

serves 8–10

Preheat the oven to 150°C (300°F) Gas 2.

In a large bowl, whisk the egg whites with the salt until stiff peaks form. Gradually, one spoonful at a time, add the sugar, whisking between each addition. The mixture should be thick and glossy. Whisk in the cornflour/cornstarch and vinegar before whisking in the vanilla.

Spoon generous dollops of the mixture in a ring shape about 25 cm/10 in. in diameter on to the prepared baking sheet. Spoon more of the mixture in the middle and build up the sides slightly higher. Make swirls in the pavlova with a fork an attractive finish. Put in the oven, close the oven door and immediately reduce the temperature to 140°C (275°F) Gas 1. Bake the pavlova for 1 hour.

Turn the oven off, but leave the pavlova inside, with the oven door shut, until the oven is cold. It's easiest to make this stage in the evening and leave in the oven overnight to cool.

To make the elderflower cream, whisk the cream until stiff but not dry, before adding the cordial. Taste for flavour, adding a little more if you want to.

Place the pavlova on a serving plate and spread the elderflower cream thickly over the top, then pile the fruit on top. Tuck a few sprigs of mint in between the fruit for extra colour contrast if you want to. Dust with icing/confectioners' sugar immediately before serving.

Battenberg Cake

This cake has featured in British recipe books for over 200 years and its distinctive name is thought to be in honour of Princess Victoria's marriage to Prince Louis of Battenberg in 1884.

175 g/³⁄₄ cup plus
   2 tablespoons
   caster/granulated
   sugar
175 g/1¹⁄₂ sticks
   unsalted butter,
   softened
3 eggs
50 g/¹⁄₃ cup ground
   almonds
125 g self-raising/rising
   flour, sifted
1 teaspoon baking
   powder
a pinch of salt
1 tablespoon pure
   vanilla extract
a few drops of pink
   food dye
1 quantity marzipan
   (see page 11)
100 g/scant ¹⁄₂ cup
   apricot jam/jelly
   (see page 11)
icing/confectioners'
   sugar, to dust

*a 20-cm/8-in. square
cake pan, greased and
lined with baking
parchment*

serves 8–10

Preheat the oven to 180°C (350°F) Gas 4.

Take a piece of foil 80 cm/32 in. long and fold it in half to make it double strength. Measure 10 cm/4 in. from the left and fold the foil. Create a 10-cm/4-in. pleat by folding the foil back towards your left hand and then back towards your right hand. Trim the foil so that it is 20-cm/8-in. wide. Grease the foil and snugly fit it in the cake pan. You should be left with two 10-cm/4-in. compartments, one for the white cake and one for the pink cake.

To make the cake, put all the ingredients, except for the pink food dye, in a large mixing bowl and whisk together for a couple of minutes, or until smooth and creamy. Spoon half the cake batter into one of the compartments in the prepared pan. Add pink food dye to remaining cake batter and mix in before spooning it into the remaining half of the pan. Level the tops of each half of the cake batter with a palette knife.

Bake for 20–25 minutes, or until an inserted skewer comes out clean. Leave the cakes to cool in the pan for 10 minutes before turning out on to a wire rack to cool completely.

In the meantime, make the marzipan following the instructions on page 11.

To assemble, trim off any brown edges off the cakes with a long serrated knife. Put one sponge cake layer on top of the other to double-check they are the same size. Trim if necessary. Cut each sponge in half lengthways.

Warm the jam/jelly in a saucepan over a gentle heat and push it through a sieve/strainer. Brush some jam/jelly along one side of a thin rectangle of white cake and stick a rectangle of the pink cake next to it. Brush the top of the white cake with jam/jelly and stick a rectangle of pink on top of it. Brush jam/jelly over the top of the pink cake on the base level and the side of the pink cake on the top level. Stick the final piece of white cake to complete the checkerboard effect.

Next, dust the work surface with the icing/confectioners' sugar and roll out the marzipan and trim it, so you are left with a rectangle of 40.5 x 23 cm/16 x 9 in., with the narrowest edge facing towards you. Brush jam/jelly on the base of the cake and stick it to the edge of the marzipan closest to you. Brush the top and sides of the cake with more jam/jelly and roll it carefully until the cake is entirely encased in marzipan.

Press the edges of the marzipan together and turn it over so that the join is at the base of the cake. Next, trim off the excess marzipan at the ends to create a neat finish. Gently score the top of the cake to make a diamond pattern before dusting with icing/confectioners sugar.

Sachertorte (Austrian Chocolate Cake)

250 g/8 oz. dark/ bittersweet chocolate, broken into pieces

6 large eggs, separated

200 g/1 cup caster/ granulated sugar

150 g/1 cup ground almonds

2 teaspoons freshly ground coffee

½ teaspoon salt

2 tablespoons apricot jam/jelly (see page 11)

For the glaze

150 g/5 oz. dark/ bittersweet chocolate, coarsely chopped

150 ml/²/₃ cup single/ light cream

25 g/2 tablespoons unsalted butter, softened

a 23-cm/9-in. loose- bottomed round cake pan, greased and lined with baking parchment

serves 10–12

Preheat the oven to 180°C (350°F) Gas 4.

To make the cake, melt the chocolate in a heatproof bowl suspended over a pan of barely simmering water. Take the bowl off the heat and leave to cool slightly.

In the meantime, whisk the egg yolks and sugar in a large mixing bowl until pale and mousse-like. Whisk in the cooled melted chocolate and mix in the ground almonds and coffee.

In a separate bowl, whisk the egg whites with the salt until stiff peaks forms. Vigorously beat one-third of the egg whites into the chocolate mixture, before gently folding in the rest with a large metal spoon.

Turn into prepared pan and bake for 45–55 minutes, or until an inserted skewer comes out clean. If the top is browning too quickly, you can cover it with foil halfway through the baking time. Leave the cake to cool completely in its pan on top of a wire rack before turning out. Put the cake on top of a wire rack with a sheet of baking parchment underneath to catch drips.

Warm the jam/jelly in a saucepan over a gentle heat and brush it over the top and sides of the cake.

To make the chocolate glaze, put the chocolate in a heatproof bowl. Heat the cream in a saucepan over a gentle heat almost to boiling, tiny bubbles should appear around the edge. Remove the pan from the heat. Pour the cream over the chocolate and leave to stand for 1 minute. Add the butter and mix everything together until melted, thick and glossy.

Pour the chocolate glaze over the cake and spread it over the top and sides of the cake. Leave to set for 30 minutes–1 hour before transferring to a serving plate.

This cake will keep in an airtight container for up to a week.

This Viennese torte was created in 1832 when Prince Wenzel Matternich called for a special dessert to be created for an important function. Franz Sacher, a trainee pastry chef, invented the cake. He passed on the recipe to his eldest son, Eduard, who developed it for the Demel Bakery and later served it in his Sacher Hotel from 1876. The Sacher Hotel to this day has queues of eager customers at its door, keen to try this famous Austrian dessert.

Pastries

Treacle Tart

This beloved British tart was created in the 1880s with the invention of golden/light corn syrup, but similar recipes using black treacle can be traced back to the 17th century. I add a little honey for depth of flavour, but you can substitute it for more golden/light corn syrup if you prefer.

For the pastry

100 g/6½ tablespoons unsalted butter
80 g/½ cup plus 1 tablespoon icing/confectioners' sugar, sifted
200 g/1⅔ cups plain/all-purpose flour, sifted, plus extra for dusting
seeds of 1 vanilla pod
finely grated zest of 1 unwaxed lemon
2 egg yolks
a pinch of salt
1 tablespoon whole milk
1 egg, beaten, for brushing

For the filling

50 g/3 tablespoons butter
300 g/1¼ cups golden/light corn syrup
100 g/scant ½ cup clear runny honey
50 ml/3 tablespoons double/heavy cream
finely grated zest and juice of 1 lemon
1 egg
1 egg yolk
85 g/1¼ cups brioche/challah crumbs
¼ teaspoon salt

clotted cream, to serve

a food processor
a 25-cm/10-in. loose bottomed tart pan

serves 4–6

To make the pastry, put all the ingredients, except the milk and beaten egg, in a food processor and blitz until the mixture resembles breadcrumbs. Add the milk and blitz until the pastry starts to form a dough, but don't overwork it. Wrap the dough in clingfilm/plastic wrap and put in the fridge for at least 30 minutes.

Preheat the oven to 180°C (350°F) Gas 4.

Roll out the pastry between two sheets of clingfilm/plastic wrap until it is about 1 cm/³⁄₁₆ in. thick and line the tart pan. Gently press the pastry into the edges of the pan, slicing the overhanging edges off with your thumb. Leave to chill in the fridge for 20 minutes. Line the pastry case with baking parchment and fill with baking beans before blind baking for 20 minutes. Remove the pan from the oven, remove the baking beans and parchment, brush the pastry base with a little of the beaten egg and put back in the oven for 5 minutes.

To make the filling, melt the butter and syrup together in a pan over a medium heat. Take the pan off the heat and stir in the remaining ingredients. Pour the mixture into the tart case and bake for 25 minutes. Reduce the oven temperature to 140°C (275°F) Gas 1 and bake for a further 20 minutes or until set.

Leave the tart to cool for a couple of hours before removing it from its pan. This is delicious served with clotted/extra thick cream.

Bakewell Tart

This traditional Derbyshire tart makes for a delicious end to a long and lazy Sunday lunch, served warm from the oven – for those who, like me, are too impatient to wait for it to cool – with a generous dollop of thick cream.

125 g/1 stick unsalted butter
100 g/⅔ cup icing/confectioners' sugar, sifted
200 g/1⅔ cups plain/all-purpose flour, sifted
25 g/2½ tablespoons ground almonds
2 egg yolks
1 beaten egg
seeds of 1 vanilla pod
a pinch of salt
2 tablespoons whole milk
50 g/½ cup flaked/slivered almonds

For the filling
300 g/1¼ cups raspberry jam/jelly (see page 11)
250 g/2 sticks unsalted butter
250 g/1¼ cups caster/granulated sugar
275 g/1¾ cups ground almonds
2 large eggs, beaten
seeds of 1 vanilla pod
50 g/⅓ cup plus 1 tablespoon plain/all-purpose flour
a pinch of salt
1 tablespoon almond liqueur

a food processor
a 20-cm/8-in. square tart pan

serves 8–10

Put all the shortcrust pastry ingredients, except the milk and beaten egg, in a food processor and blitz until the mixture resembles breadcrumbs. Add the milk and blitz until the pastry starts to form a dough, but don't overwork it. Wrap the dough in clingfilm/plastic wrap and put in the fridge to rest for at least 1 hour.

Preheat the oven to 180°C (350°F) Gas 4.

Roll out the pastry in between two sheets of clingfilm/plastic wrap (this will stop you using too much flour when rolling out the pastry). Remove the top layer of clingfilm/plastic wrap and upturn the sheet of pastry over the tart pan and press into the edges. Remove the clingfilm/plastic wrap, prick the pastry base with a fork and slice the overhanging edges of pastry off with your thumb. Line with baking parchment,

fill with baking beans and blind bake for 15–20 minutes. Remove from the oven, remove the baking beans and parchment, brush the pastry base with a little of the beaten egg and return to the oven for 5 minutes. Leave to cool.

Spread the jam/jelly over the base of the pastry case. Next, make the frangipane filling. Whisk the butter and sugar until light and fluffy. Add the almonds, eggs, vanilla, flour and almond liqueur and whisk until fully incorporated and smooth. Spoon the mixture on top of the jam/jelly and level the top with a palette knife.

Decorate the top with the flaked/slivered almonds and bake for 40–45 minutes, or until the filling is firm and golden. Leave to cool slightly before taking the tart out of the pan.

Mississippi Mud Pie

This 20th-century American sweet pie hails from Mississippi. The dense chocolate cake baked in a cookie crust is supposed to resemble the banks of the Mississippi River.

For the crust
400 g/14 oz. chocolate biscuits or cookies (dark/bittersweet chocolate digestives are good)
80 g/5 tablespoons unsalted butter, melted

For the cake
175 g/6 oz. dark/bittersweet chocolate, broken into pieces
125 g/1 stick unsalted butter, cut into cubes
3 eggs, separated
½ teaspoon salt
1 teaspoon ground espresso coffee beans
20 g/2½ tablespoons ground almonds
20 g/2½ tablespoons plain/all-purpose flour, sifted

For the mousse
225 g/15 oz. dark/bittersweet chocolate, broken into pieces
150 g/1 stick plus 2 tablespoons unsalted butter

5 eggs, separated
85 g/⅔ cup icing/confectioners' sugar
a pinch of salt
135 ml/½ cup plus 1 tablespoon double/heavy cream

For the topping
300 ml/1¼ cups double/heavy cream
50 g/⅓ cup icing/confectioners' sugar
1 teaspoon pure vanilla extract
50 g/1½ oz. dark/bittersweet chocolate shavings

a food processor
a 20-cm/8-in. springform cake pan, greased and base lined with baking parchment
a chefs' blow torch (optional)

serves 8–10

To make the crust, blitz the biscuits/cookies until crumbs in a food processor. Pour in the butter and pulse until the mixture has combined. Tip into the prepared pan and press it down firmly, taking it halfway up the sides of the pan. Chill in the fridge for about 1 hour. Preheat the oven to 160°C (325°F) Gas 3. Bake the crust for 10 minutes, remove from the oven and leave to cool. Increase the oven temperature to 180°C (350°F) Gas 4.

To make the mud cake, melt the chocolate in a large heatproof bowl suspended over a pan of simmering water, stirring occasionally. Take the bowl off the heat and stir in the butter until it has melted. In a separate bowl, whisk the egg whites and salt together to stiff peaks and set aside. Whisk the egg yolks into the melted chocolate, one at a time. Mix in the coffee, ground almonds and flour. Vigorously beat in one-third of the egg whites to slacken the mixture. Fold the remaining egg whites into the chocolate batter with a large metal spoon. Pour the mixture into the cooled crust and bake for 30 minutes.

To make the mud mousse, melt the chocolate and butter as above. Whisk in the egg yolks, one at a time. Sift over the icing/confectioners' sugar and mix in. In another bowl, whisk the egg whites with the salt to stiff peaks. Set aside while you whisk the cream to stiff peaks. Fold the cream into the chocolate mixture. Next, fold in the egg whites using a large metal spoon. Pour the mousse over the top of the cold mud cake and chill in the fridge for at least 8 hours. Once the mousse has set, run a blow torch (or a hot sharp knife) around the edges to release the pie from the pan. Put on a plate.

Whisk the cream until stiff. Sift in the icing/confectioners' sugar and mix. Add the vanilla extract and whisk again. Spread the cream over the mousse and decorate with chocolate shavings.

Pecan Pie

Created by French immigrants living in New Orleans, this delicious sweet pie has become a favourite American dessert which is particularly popular as a Thanksgiving celebration staple. Perfect served with a generous dollop of whipped cream.

For the pastry

250 g/2 cups plain/
    all-purpose flour
a pinch of salt
100 g/³/₄ cups plus 1
    tablespoon icing/
    confectioners' sugar
100 g/6½ tablespoons
    cold unsalted butter,
    cut into cubes
2 eggs
seeds of 1 vanilla pod
    (optional)

For the filling

75 g/5 tablespoons
    unsalted butter
225 g/1 cup plus 2
    tablespoons light
    muscovado sugar
325 g/1⅓ cups maple
    syrup
½ teaspoon salt
225 g/1½ cups pecans
2 tablespoons bourbon
2 teaspoons pure vanilla
    extract
3 eggs, lightly beaten

a food processor
a 23-cm/9-in. loose-
    bottomed tart pan

serves 8–10

To make the pastry, blitz the flour, salt and icing/confectioners' sugar together in a food processor to combine. Add the butter and pulse until the mixture resembles fine breadcrumbs. Add the eggs and vanilla, if using, and pulse again until just incorporated. Scoop the dough out of the mixer and wrap it in a large sheet of clingfilm/plastic wrap. Put it in the fridge to rest for at least 1 hour.

Preheat the oven to 180°C (350°F) Gas 4.

Roll the pastry between two sheets of clingfilm/plastic wrap until it is about 1 cm/³/₁₆ in. thick. Take off the top layer of clingfilm/plastic wrap and upturn the pastry into the tart pan. Gently press the pastry into the edges of the pan, slicing the overhanging edges off with your thumb. Remove the top layer of clingfilm/plastic wrap and prick the base with a fork. Put the tart case in the freezer for 15 minutes to chill.

Line the pastry case with baking parchment and fill with baking beans. Bake in the oven for 15 minutes. Remove the baking beans and baking parchment and return to the oven for a further 5 minutes.

While the pastry case is baking, make the filling. Put the butter, sugar, maple syrup and salt in a saucepan and stir over a medium heat until the butter has melted and the sugar has dissolved. Turn the heat up and bring the mixture to the boil. Take the pan off the heat and mix in the pecans, the bourbon and vanilla and leave to cool for a few minutes. Whisk the eggs into the slightly cooled mixture until completely combined and pour the filling into the tart case. Bake for 40–45 minutes.

Leave the pie to cool in its pan on a wire rack before unmoulding. Serve warm or at room temperature.

Melktert

Afrikaans for 'milk tart', this South African dessert is light, fluffy and delicious. With a higher ratio of milk than in custard tarts, melktert is less rich, so that second slice feels less sinful.

For the pastry

100 g/6½ tablespoons unsalted butter, softened
100 g/½ cup caster/granulated sugar
1 egg
2 teaspoons pure vanilla extract
200 g/1⅔ cups plain/all-purpose flour
a pinch of salt

For the filling

1 vanilla pod/bean
600 ml/2½ cups whole milk
1 cinnamon stick
4 eggs, separated
100 g/½ cup caster/granulated sugar
25 g/2½ tablespoons plain/all-purpose flour
25 g/2½ tablespoons cornflour
30 g/2 tablespoons unsalted butter, cut into cubes
a pinch of salt
½ teaspoon ground cinnamon
2 teaspoons caster/granulated sugar

a 23-cm/9-in. tart pan, greased

serves 8–10

To make the pastry base, cream the butter and sugar together in a large bowl until soft and creamy. Whisk in the egg, followed by the vanilla, then sift over the flour. Add the salt and mix thoroughly. Roughly press the mixture into the base of the prepared pan and up the sides. Prick the base and put the pastry case in the freezer for 15 minutes or in the refrigerator for 30 minutes to chill.

Preheat the oven to 180°C (350°F) Gas 4. Bake for 25–30 minutes. Leave to cool on a wire rack.

To make the filling, split the vanilla pod and scrape out the seeds. Put the milk, vanilla pod and seeds and cinnamon stick in a saucepan over a gentle heat. Leave to infuse for 5–10 minutes, before increasing the heat and scalding the milk (see page 8).

In the meantime, whisk the egg yolks, sugar and flours together until smooth. Take the milk mixture off the heat, strain into the egg mixture, discarding the vanilla pod/bean and cinnamon stick and whisk together. Quickly rinse out the saucepan before pouring the mixture back in.

Stir the custard over a medium heat until thickened – this can take a few minutes, so be patient. Once thick, stir in the butter until melted and transfer the mixture to a large jug/pitcher or bowl. Leave to cool slightly.

In a spotlessly clean bowl, whisk together the egg whites and salt until stiff peaks form. Fold the egg whites into the warm custard and, once fully combined, pour the mixture into the prepared tart case. Mix the cinnamon and sugar together and sprinkle over the top.

Leave to cool to room temperature before transferring to the fridge to set for a few hours.

Crumbly shortcrust pastry filled with a tangy lemon curd filling, topped with billowing meringue, lemon meringue pie is a real favourite of so many. Lemons have been used in European desserts since medieval times, but lemon meringue pie as we know it today, evolved with the invention of meringue in the 18th century.

Lemon Meringue Pie

For the pastry

80 g/½ cup icing/
   confectioners' sugar
180 g/1⅓ cups plain/
   all-purpose flour
100 g/6½ tablespoons
   unsalted cold butter,
   cut into cubes
1 egg, separated
1 tablespoon cold whole
   milk
a pinch of salt
finely grated zest of
   1 unwaxed lemon
beaten egg white,
   to seal

For the filling

3 tablespoons
   cornflour/cornstarch
finely grated zest of 5
   unwaxed lemons
juice of 6 lemons
100 g/½ cup caster/
   granulated sugar
50 g/3 tablespoons
   unsalted butter,
   cut into cubes
4 egg yolks
1 egg
1 quantity meringue
   (see page 9)

a food processor
a 23-cm/9-in. loose-
   bottomed tart pan
a large piping bag fitted
   with a large star-
   shaped nozzle/tip
   (optional)

serves 8–10

Blitz the icing/confectioners' sugar and flour in a flood processor until well mixed. Add the cubes of butter and pulse until the mixture resembles fine breadcrumbs. Add the egg yolk, milk, salt and lemon zest and pulse again until just combined. Tip the soft dough on to a sheet of clingfilm/plastic wrap, wrap it up and put it in the fridge to rest for at least 30 minutes.

Put the shortcrust pastry between two sheets of clingfilm/plastic wrap before rolling it out to about 5 mm/¼ in. thick. Remove the top layer of clingfilm/plastic wrap and turn the pastry over into the tart pan and gently push the pastry into place with your thumbs. Use your thumb to slice off any overhanging pastry and carefully peel off the clingfilm/plastic wrap. Prick the base with a fork and put it in the fridge to chill until firm.

Preheat the oven to 180°C (350°F) Gas 4.

Line the pastry with baking parchment – I find the easiest way to do this is to crumple the paper roughly before sitting it snugly inside the tart case – and cover with baking beans. Blind bake the pastry in the oven for 20 minutes. Remove the baking beans and baking parchment and brush the pastry with beaten egg white. Return in the oven for 5 minutes, then remove and put on a wire rack while you make the lemon curd filling.

Reduce the oven temperature to 160°C (325°F) Gas 3.

To make the lemon curd filling, put the cornflour/cornstarch,

150 ml/⅔ cup water and caster/granulated sugar in a saucepan and stir until it forms a paste. Add the lemon juice and zest and stir over a medium heat until the mixture has thickened. Take the pan off the heat and whisk in the butter until it has melted. Leave to cool for a couple of minutes. Whisk together the egg yolks and egg and whisk into the lemon mixture. Return the pan to the heat and continue to whisk for 3–4 minutes until the lemon curd has thickened enough to dollop. Set aside while you make the meringue topping following the instructions on page 9.

To assemble the pie, pour the lemon curd filling into the pastry case and level it with a palette knife. You can, if you wish, pipe the meringue on top using a large star-shaped nozzle, but a simple tablespoon and a fork will suffice. Start by piping or spooning a ring of meringue around the very edge of the filling, to create a seal between the meringue and the pastry that will prevent the curd leaking out.

Next, billow the remaining meringue over the top of the rest of the pie and, if not using a piping bag, create a few wispy flourishes by swirling a fork in the top. Bake for 25–30 minutes or until the meringue is firm and slightly golden. Leave the pie to cool in its pan completely before removing. Lemon meringue pie is always best eaten on the day it is baked.

Maids of Honour Tarts

These dainty curd tarts date back to Tudor England and are said to have been a particular favourite of Henry VIII. They are thought to have been named after the maids of honour who served at Richmond Palace in the 16th century and are sometimes known as Richmond tarts. Whatever you choose to call them, they are a wonderful afternoon treat, served warm from the oven.

500 g/16 oz. ready-made puff pastry
icing/confectioners' sugar, for dusting

For the filling
250 g/1 cup ricotta
75 g/$\frac{1}{3}$ cup caster/granulated sugar
finely grated zest of 2 unwaxed lemons
juice of 1 lemon
50 g/$\frac{1}{3}$ cup ground almonds
a pinch of salt
3 eggs
3 tablespoons lemon curd

a 8-cm/3½-in. round cutter with a fluted edge
2 x 12-hole muffin pans, greased

makes 24

Preheat the oven to 200°C (400°F) Gas 6.

Begin by making the filling, whisk together all the ingredients, except for the lemon curd and icing/confectioners' sugar, until completely smooth.

Dust the work surface with flour and roll the pastry to a thickness of about 3 mm/$\frac{1}{8}$ in. Dip the cutter in flour and stamp out 24 circles. Be careful not to twist the cutter as it may affect the rise of the pastry. Do not re-knead and re-roll leftover pastry as the layers will be ruined and it will not rise properly, so make sure you stamp the discs out closely together. Drape a pastry disc over each hole in the muffin pans before gently pushing each one into the holes.

Put a scant teaspoon of lemon curd into the base of each tart. Next, put a scant tablespoon of the ricotta mixture on top. Put the muffin pans in the oven and bake for 20–25 minutes or until golden and nicely risen.

Once cool enough to handle, transfer the tarts to a wire rack to cool completely. Sift a little icing/confectioners' sugar over each tart before serving.

Banoffee Pie

I have a real soft spot for this nursery-sweet, British classic based on the flavours of toffee and banana. My late, beloved grandfather once declared his slice of banoffee pie to be 'bamboozlingly delicious'. This dessert really is astonishingly simple to make, especially considering its irresistible charms. The toffee in my banoffee omits the traditional, dangerous (and, at times, literally explosive) practice of boiling a can of condensed milk for most of a day. So, you can breathe a sigh of relief that, aside from the calorie count, this recipe is entirely risk free.

250 g/8 oz. digestive
   biscuits/graham
   crackers
140 g/1 stick plus
   1 tablespoon butter
1 x 397-g/14-oz. can
   condensed milk
75 g/⅓ cup dark
   muscovado sugar
2 teaspoons pure
   vanilla extract
3 bananas
300 ml/1¼ cups
   double/heavy cream
25 g/1 oz.
   dark/bittersweet
   chocolate, grated

a food processor
6 individual loose-
*   bottomed tart cases*

makes 6

Preheat the oven to 180°C (350°F) Gas 4.

Melt 65 g/5 tablespoons of the butter. Blitz the biscuits in a food processor until completely crushed, add the melted butter and pulse until fully combined. Press the buttery biscuit rubble firmly into the base and sides of the tart pan. Bake for 10 minutes to set and leave to cool completely on a wire rack.

While the biscuit base is cooling, put the condensed milk, sugar, vanilla and the remaining butter in a saucepan. Stir over a gentle heat until the butter has melted and the sugar has dissolved. Increase the heat and bring to the boil, stirring all the time, for a few minutes, until thick and golden. Pour the toffee sauce over the biscuit base and leave to cool. Once completely cold, transfer to the fridge for at least 1 hour to set.

Carefully remove the tart case and transfer the pie to a serving plate. Slice the bananas and arrange them over the toffee in an even layer. Whip the cream to soft peaks and spread over the layer of bananas. Swirl the cream with a fork to create a more attractive finish, before scattering over the chocolate.

Éclairs with chantilly cream filling

The word 'éclair' roughly translates as 'flash of lightning', but these elegant 19th-century French pastries were known as *pains à la duchesse* until 1850. They are made from featherlight choux/cream puff pastry filled with whipped cream or sometimes crème pâtissière and, despite their impressive appearance, are wonderfully simple to make. This recipe offers a choice of two glazes to top your éclairs.

For the pastry
75 g/5 tablespoons butter, cut into cubes
100 g/³⁄₄ cup plain/all-purpose flour, sifted
a pinch of salt
3 large eggs, beaten

For the filling
300 ml/1¹⁄₄ cups double/heavy cream
2 tablespoons icing/confectioners' sugar, sifted
2 teaspoons pure vanilla extract

For the chocolate glaze
50 g/1¹⁄₂ oz. dark/bittersweet chocolate
1 tablespoon whole milk
1 tablespoon icing/confectioners' sugar

For the coffee glaze
225 g/1¹⁄₂ cups icing/confectioners' sugar
2 tablespoons coffee

2 large piping bags fitted with plain nozzles/tips
2 baking sheets, lined with baking parchment

makes 12

Preheat the oven to 220°C (425°F) Gas 7.

Put 150 ml/²⁄₃ cup water in a saucepan or pot with the butter over a medium heat. Stir until the butter has melted and then increase the heat and bring to a rolling boil, then immediately remove from the heat. Shoot in the flour and salt and beat vigorously until the mixture comes together. Put the saucepan or pot back over a gentle heat, stirring for 1 minute. Remove from the heat and leave to cool for 5 minutes.

Using a wooden spoon, add a little of the egg at a time, beating very well in between each addition until you have a soft, silky batter with a dropping consistency. You may not need all the egg.

Put the mixture in one of the prepared piping bags. Pipe 12 lines of pastry, each about 15 cm/6 in. long, on to the prepared baking sheets. Use a wet finger to pat down any peaks.

Bake in the oven for 20–25 minutes or until the éclairs have puffed up and golden. Remove from the oven and stab the base of each éclair with a skewer to allow the steam to escape. Return to the baking sheet and put them back in the oven for 5 minutes. Turn the oven off and open the door and leave the éclairs in there for another 5 minutes before transferring to a wire rack to cool.

Once the éclairs are completely cold, make the Chantilly cream by whisking the cream until stiff before whisking in the sifted icing sugar and vanilla extract to taste. Fill the second prepared piping bag with the Chantilly cream. Press the tip of the nozzle into the hole in the base of an éclair and gently squeeze the base of the piping bag until the éclair is filled. Repeat with the remaining éclairs until they are all filled.

To make the chocolate glaze, melt the chocolate and milk together in a heatproof bowl suspended over a pan of barely simmering water. Once the chocolate has melted, simply whisk in the sifted icing/confectioners' sugar to sweeten.

To make the coffee glaze, whisk the espresso coffee into the sifted icing/confectioners' sugar.

Dip each éclair with into your chosen glaze, or spread some of the glaze over the top of each éclair. Alternatively, you can halve the quantities given for the glazes and ice half with the coffee glaze and half with the chocolate glaze.

Eccles Cakes

These Lancashire pastries hail from the town of Eccles and are affectionately known as 'squashed fly cakes' because of the currant filling. 'Eccles' means 'church' and Eccles cakes were eaten during religious festivals. Oliver Cromwell banned these pastries in 1653 because of their frivolity and apparent connection to paganism but their popularity has endured.

For the pastry
400 g/3 cups plus 2 tablespoons plain/all-purpose flour, plus extra for dusting
½ teaspoon salt
250 g/2 sticks cold butter, cut into small cubes
freshly squeezed juice of ½ lemon

For the filling
75 g/5 tablespoons butter
200 g/1⅓ cups dried (Zante) currants
150 g/¾ cup light muscovado sugar
1 teaspoon ground cinnamon
½ teaspoon grated nutmeg
¼ teaspoon ground cloves
finely grated zest and juice of 1 lemon
finely grated zest of 1 orange

For the glaze
2–3 tablespoons whole milk
1 egg, beaten
2 tablespoons demerara sugar

2 baking sheets, lined with baking parchment
a 10-cm/4-in. round cookie cutter

makes 10

To make the pastry, sift the flour and salt into a large bowl. Rub half the butter into the flour with your fingertips until it resembles fine breadcrumbs. Add the lemon juice and 6 tablespoons fridge-cold water. Use a fork to bring the mixture together into a dough – you may need to add a little more water. Dust the work surface with flour, tip the dough out and roll it out to a 20 x 30-cm/8 x 12-in. rectangle. Dot the remaining butter over the dough and fold the two ends into the middle, then fold it in half. Wrap the pastry in clingfilm/ plastic wrap and rest it in the fridge for 15 minutes, before rolling again, folding and resting three more times. Wrap again and rest in the fridge for at least 45 minutes.

To make the filling, put all the ingredients in a saucepan set over medium heat. Stir until the butter has melted then boil until slightly thickened.

Preheat the oven to 200°C (400°F) Gas 6.

Dust the work surface with flour and roll the dough out to the thickness of about 3 mm/⅛ in. Use the cutter to stamp out 10 discs. Do not be tempted to twist the cutter, as it may affect the rise of the cakes. Put a tablespoon of the filling in the centre of each disc. Brush the edges of a disc with beaten egg, gather the edges together and squeeze to seal. Turn over and lightly roll until flat. Make three slashes across the top with a sharp knife. Repeat with the remaining pastry discs.

Transfer the Eccles cakes to the prepared baking sheets. Mix the milk with the beaten egg and brush the top of each one. Sprinkle with demerara sugar and bake for 15–20 minutes, until golden and well risen. Transfer to a wire rack to cool completely.

Mince Pies

250 g/2 cups plain/all-purpose flour, sifted
a pinch of salt
100 g/6½ tablespoons cold unsalted butter, cut into cubes
100 g/½ cup caster/granulated sugar
2 eggs, beaten
1 tablespoon icing/confectioners' sugar, for dusting

a 12-hole muffin pan
a 10-cm/4-in. round cookie cutter
a 5-cm/2-in. star-shaped cookie cutter

makes 12

For the mincemeat

125 g/1 medium apple, cored and finely diced
100 g/3½ oz. damsons or other plums, pitted and finely chopped
110 g/3½ oz. shredded beef or vegetarian suet
110 g/⅔ cup (dark) raisins
110 g/⅔ cup sultanas/golden raisins
110 g/⅔ cup currants
80 g/½ cup dried sour cherries
50 g/⅓ cup dried cranberries
180 g/scant 1 cup dark muscovado sugar
finely grated zest and juice of 1 large orange
finely grated zest and juice of 2 lemons
75 g/½ cup chopped fresh hazelnuts or almonds
1 teaspoon mixed spice/apple pie spice
1 teaspoon ground cinnamon
a pinch of ground cloves
½ teaspoon grated nutmeg
200 ml/¾ cup brandy

makes 1.5 kg/3 lbs.

Preheat the oven to 120°C (250°F) Gas ½.

To make the mincemeat, put all the ingredients except the brandy in a large heatproof bowl and thoroughly mix. Cover with foil and cook in the oven for 3½ hours. Remove from the oven and stir. Leave to cool, stirring every now and then until the mixture is completely cold. Stir in the brandy. Spoon into a large sterilized jar (see page 4), top with a disc of waxed paper and cover with a new lid and clean screw band. Process for 15 minutes in a boiling water bath or store in the fridge.

Store the mincemeat in a cool, dark place. The flavours will improve after a month or two, but the mincemeat will last up to a year. This makes far more than is needed for 12 mince pies, but it will be just enough to last the Christmas period and all the mulled wine and mince pie parties. Once opened, store the mincemeat in the fridge.

To make the pastry, sift the flour into a large bowl and stir in the salt. Add the butter and rub the butter into the flour with your fingertips. Stir in the sugar and make a well in the middle of the bowl. Add half the beaten egg and use a fork to mix the dry ingredients into the wet. Tip the mixture out on to a lightly floured surface and lightly knead until it comes together into a dough. Wrap in clingfilm/plastic wrap and put in the fridge to chill for at least 30 minutes.

Preheat the oven to 200°C (375°F) Gas 5.

Dust the work surface with flour and roll the pastry out no thicker than ½ cm/³⁄₁₆ inch. Use the round cutter to stamp out 12 pastry discs. Line the muffin pan with the pastry discs and generously fill each one with mincemeat. Bring the rest of the pastry back together and re-roll. Use the star-shaped cutter to stamp out 12 stars and rest one on each pie to make an attractive lid. Brush the top of each pie with a little of the remaining beaten egg and bake for 15–20 minutes, or until the pies are golden brown. Leave the pies to cool before taking them out of the pan. Lightly dust the mince pies with icing/confectioners' sugar.

Spiced meat pies have been enjoyed in England since the 12th century when Crusaders returned to British soil with Middle Eastern spices. Originally, they contained meat as well as spiced fruits, but now, they only contain dried fruit and lots of booze.

Desserts & Puddings

Spotted Dick

A school dinner staple for British winters, the name 'Spotted Dick' has long been a curse to acne-prone boys called Richard! The first recorded recipe for this steamed suet pudding appears in 1849 and the unusual name owes nothing to to spotty-faced schoolboys. It is thought that 'spotted' refers to the liberal use of currants and that 'dick' may actually be a corruption of the word 'dough'. You can make four small puddings (as shown) if preferred.

250 g/2 cups plain/
    all-purpose flour
2 teaspoons baking
    powder
a pinch of salt
175 g/1 heaping cup
    dried (Zante) currants
75 g/⅓ cup caster/
    granulated sugar
finely grated zest of
    2 lemons
125 g/4 oz. (¾ cup)
    shredded beef or
    vegetarian suet
200 ml/¾ cup plus
    2 tablespoons whole
    milk
custard sauce (see page
    10), to serve

a 1.2-litre/2-pint
    pudding basin,
    generously greased
kitchen string
a steamer

serves 6

Sift the flour and baking powder into a large mixing bowl. Add the salt, currants, sugar, lemon zest and suet and mix together. Stir in the milk to make a sticky dough. Spoon the mixture into the prepared pudding basin and level the top.

Lay a large piece of foil on the work surface and an equal-size piece of greaseproof paper on top. Fold a pleat in both together and place over the top of the bowl. Pat down the sides and tie a very long piece of kitchen string tightly around the rim of the pudding basin to secure it. Take the excess string and pass it over the top of the bowl and secure the end to the knot around the rim. This will act as a handle to remove the pudding from the steamer later.

Put the basin into a steamer. Steam for 1½ –2 hours, checking the water level every now and then to ensure the pan does not boil dry.

When you are ready to serve, run a knife round the top of the pudding to release it and upturn the pudding basin on to a serving plate. Give the base a sharp tap with a wooden spoon to release the pudding. Serve piping hot with lashings of hot custard sauce.

Jam Roly Poly

A favourite school dinner staple, this old-fashioned British pudding is hearty winter fare. Often affectionately known as dead man's arm, because of its log shape and oozing raspberry jam/jelly, this pud is made with suet and steamed. It is perfect generously doused with hot custard sauce.

250 g/2 cups self-raising/rising flour, plus extra for dusting
25 g/2 tablespoons cold unsalted butter, cut into small cubes
a pinch of salt
1 tablespoon caster/granulated sugar

75 g/2½ oz. (½ cup) shredded beef or vegetarian suet
160 ml/⅔ cup whole milk
150 g/⅔ cup raspberry jam/jelly (see page 11)

a roasting pan
kitchen string

serves 6–8

Preheat the oven to 180°C (350°F) Gas 4. Put a roasting pan in the bottom of the oven to heat up, with an oven shelf directly above it.

Sift the flour into a large bowl. Rub the butter in with your fingertips. Stir the salt, sugar and suet into the flour. Make a well in the middle and add most of the milk (you may not need it all). Use a fork to mix the dry ingredients into the wet until it makes a sticky dough. Tip the dough on to a lightly floured surface, pat it together and dust the top with flour. Roll the dough into a square that is roughly 25 x 25 cm/10 x 10 in.

Spread the jam/jelly over the square, leaving a 1-cm/½-in. gap at the end furthest away from you. Roll the dough up into a tight sausage. Pinch along the join to seal.

Take a large sheet of baking parchment and fold a pleat into the middle. Roll the roly poly up in the parchment and twist round each end and tie with kitchen string. Repeat with a sheet of foil.

Carefully pour boiling water into the hot roasting pan about a third full. Put the roly poly on the oven shelf above the roasting pan and bake for 40–45 minutes. Carefully unwrap the pudding, cut it into thick slices and serve with lashings of hot custard sauce.

Peach Cobbler

Rustic, homely and filling, this peach cobbler makes a comforting end to any meal. This is delicious family food at its best – satisfying and perfect for sharing. If you can't get hold of peaches, you can use whatever fruit is in season. Plums, cherries and apples all work particularly well.

8 fresh peaches, peeled and stoned/pitted

50 g/¼ cup light muscovado sugar

450 g/3½ cups self-raising/rising flour

½ teaspoon salt

220 g/2 sticks cold butter, cut into cubes

140 g/¾ cup caster/granulated sugar

seeds of 1 vanilla pod

260 ml/1 generous cup buttermilk

a 25 x 20-cm/10 x 8-in. ovenproof dish

serves 6–8

Preheat the oven to 190°C (375°F) Gas 5.

Slice the peaches and arrange them in an even layer in the dish, then sprinkle over the light muscovado sugar.

In a large mixing bowl, sift together the flour and salt and rub in the butter with your fingertips. Stir through the caster/granulated sugar and vanilla and then add the buttermilk. Beat together with a wooden spoon until fully incorporated.

Drop mounds of dough off a tablespoon on top of the peaches to created a cobblestone effect. Bake in the oven for 25–30 minutes, or until the top is golden and the fruit is soft. Serve hot with vanilla ice cream or hot custard sauce, as preferred.

Apple & Blackberry Crumble

Crumble, one of the UK's favourite winter puddings, is a delicious result of World War II's food rationing. Butter, eggs and sugar were all in short supply, which resulted in pies and sponge cakes being replaced by the more humble crumble. I have jazzed up the traditional topping to include nuts and oats. Apple and blackberry filling is a particular favourite combination of mine, but rhubarb, gooseberries, plums and cherries all make delicious variations.

6 Braeburn apples (or another variety, similarly sharp and sweet)
juice of ½ lemon
350 g/12 oz. fresh blackberries
1 tablespoon caster/granulated sugar
100 g/¾ cup plain/all-purpose flour
50 g/⅓ cup ground almonds
50 g/½ cup pinhead/large steel-cut oats
a pinch of salt
seeds of 1 vanilla pod
100 g/7 tablespoons cold unsalted butter, cut into cubes

a 25-cm/10-in. round ovenproof dish

serves 8–10

Preheat the oven to 180°C (350°F) Gas 4.

Core and slice the apples. (You can peel them if you prefer, but I like the rusticity of a skin on crumble.) Toss the apples slices in the lemon juice and put them in the ovenproof dish. Scatter the blackberries on top and sprinkle over the sugar.

Put the flour, almonds, oats, salt and vanilla in a large bowl and mix together until well combined. Add the butter and rub the mixture with your fingers and thumbs until it resembles coarse breadcrumbs. Tip the crumble topping over the fruit, but do not be tempted to press it down.

Put it in the oven to bake for 35–40 minutes or until the top is golden and the fruit is soft and bubbling. Leave the crumble to cool for 15–20 minutes before serving with lashings of hot custard sauce or chilled cream, as preferred.

Sticky Toffee Pudding

The origin of the sticky toffee pudding is a sticky subject. Some say a Mrs Martin of The Old Rectory in Claughton, Lancashire, invented it, while others insist the pud is a Lake District creation from the Sharrow Bay Hotel in Ullswater. It's even been connected with the Udny Arms Hotel in Aberdeenshire and the Gait Inn in Millington, Yorkshire. Whoever is responsible for creating this glorious dessert has certainly done a great service for everyone.

300 g/10 oz. Medjool dates, stoned/pitted and roughly chopped
480 ml/2 cups fairly weak black tea
150 g/1 stick plus 2 tablespoons unsalted butter
110 g/½ cup light muscovado sugar
75 g/⅓ cup dark muscovado sugar
2 tablespoons golden/light corn syrup
3 large eggs, beaten
1 tablespoon pure vanilla extract
3 teaspoons mixed spice
265 g/2 cups plus 1 tablespoon self-raising/rising flour

2 teaspoons bicarbonate of soda/baking soda
¼ teaspoon salt
toffee sauce (see page 9), to serve

a 25-cm/10-in. square ovenproof dish, greased

serves 8–10

Preheat the oven to 180°C (350°F) Gas 4.

Put the dates and tea in a saucepan and bring to the boil. Turn the heat down and leave to simmer for 5 minutes. Take the pan off the heat and set aside. Cream the butter and sugars together in a large mixing bowl until pale and fluffy. Whisk in the syrup and gradually add the eggs, whisking well between each addition. Stir in the dates and vanilla. Sift all the dry ingredients over the top of the wet and fold together.

Pour the mixture into the prepared dish and bake in the oven for 45 minutes–1 hour, or until an inserted skewer comes out clean.

While the pudding is baking, make the toffee sauce following the instructions on page 9.

Remove the pudding from the oven, prick all over with a skewer and pour over a few tablespoons of the sticky toffee sauce. Serve hot with a pouring of chilled cream and a generous glug of sticky toffee sauce.

Apple Brown Betty

A brown betty is a traditional American dessert, with similarities to the British crumble. The perfect way to use up a glut of seasonal fruit and stale breadcrumbs, the brown betty is old-fashioned comfort food at its best.

7 slices stale brown bread

8 apples (Bramley, Granny Smith and Pink Lady are all good choices), cored, sliced and diced

juice of 1 lemon

125 g/²/₃ cup light muscovado sugar

2 teaspoons ground cinnamon (optional)

2 teaspoons pure vanilla extract

75 g/5 tablespoons unsalted butter, melted

a food processor

a 25-cm/10-in. square baking dish, greased

serves 8–10

Preheat the oven to 180°C (350°F) Gas 4.

Blitz the slices of bread in a food processor to make crumbs.

Toss the apples in the lemon juice and scatter half at the base of the prepared dish. Mix the breadcrumbs with the sugar, cinnamon (if using), vanilla and melted butter. Sprinkle half of the breadcrumbs over the apples. Scatter over the remaining apples and top with the remaining breadcrumbs.

Bake in the oven for 35–40 minutes, or until the apples are soft. If the breadcrumbs brown too quickly, you can cover the top with a sheet of foil. Serve warm with chilled cream or vanilla ice cream.

Cherry Clafoutis

This irresistible French dessert marries ripe seasonal fruit with light, sweet batter. Cherries are the most traditional choice for clafoutis, but blueberries, apricots and raspberries all make wonderful alternatives. Purists believe the cherries should not be stoned/pitted before baking, citing extra flavour as an excuse. I value my teeth more than tradition on this score, so always make mine stone/pit-free and suggest you do the same.

450 g/1 lb. ripe fresh cherries, stoned/pitted
2 tablespoons caster/granulated sugar
3–4 tablespoons Kirsch or brandy

For the batter
75 g/¹⁄₃ cup caster/granulated sugar
2 eggs
50 g/¹⁄₃ cup plus 1 tablespoon plain/all-purpose flour

125 ml/½ cup whole milk
2 teaspoons pure vanilla extract
25 g/2 tablespoons butter, melted
a pinch of salt

a 20-cm/8-in. flan or pie dish, greased and dusted with 1 tablespoon caster/superfine sugar

serves 6–8

Preheat the oven to 180°C (350°F) Gas 4.

Put the cherries, sugar and Kirsch in a bowl and leave to macerate for a few hours, or even overnight.

To make the batter, whisk together the sugar and eggs in a large mixing bowl. Sift over the flour and whisk until fully incorporated. Slowly whisk in the milk, followed by the vanilla and melted butter. Stir in the salt and tip the cherries and their juices into the batter.

Pour into the prepared dish and bake in the oven for 35–45 minutes, or until an inserted skewer comes out clean. Sprinkle over the caster/superfine sugar and serve warm, preferably with a generous pouring of chilled cream.

Queen of Puddings

Puddings requiring the soaking of breadcrumbs in milk date back to the 17th century. Monmouth pudding and, particularly, Manchester pudding have great similarities with queen of puddings. In fact, it has been said that Queen Victoria enjoyed a portion of Manchester pudding on a royal visit and so the dish was renamed in her honour. Whatever the origins of the name, this delicious dessert is certainly worthy of royalty.

600 ml/2$\frac{1}{2}$ cups whole milk

seeds of 1 vanilla pod/ bean

finely grated zest of 1 lemon

25 g/2 tablespoons butter

50 g/$\frac{1}{4}$ cup caster/ granulated sugar

3 egg yolks

100 g1$\frac{1}{2}$ cups brioche/ challah crumbs

6 tablespoons raspberry jam/jelly (see page 11)

vanilla ice cream (see page 11), to serve

For the meringue top

3 egg whites

a pinch of salt

170 g/$\frac{3}{4}$ cup caster/ superfine sugar

1 teaspoon cornflour/ cornstarch

½ teaspoon white wine vinegar

2 teaspoons pure vanilla extract

a 24-cm/9½-in. pie dish, greased

a piping bag fitted with a star-shaped nozzle/tip (optional)

serves 6–8

Preheat the oven to 170°C (325°F) Gas 3.

To make the base, put the milk, vanilla, lemon zest and butter in a saucepan over a gentle heat to warm. In the meantime, whisk the caster/ granulated sugar with the egg yolks in a large mixing bowl. When the milk is hot, but not boiling, whisk it into the egg yolks. Add the brioche/ challah crumbs to the custard and leave to soak for 15–20 minutes, to allow the crumbs to swell.

Pour the mixture into the prepared dish and bake for 30–35 minutes or until set. Remove it from the oven and spread the jam/jelly evenly over the top.

Reduce the oven temperature to 150°C (300°F) Gas 2.

In a large mixing bowl, whisk the egg whites with the salt until stiff. Gradually add the caster/superfine sugar, continuing to whisk in between each addition until you have a thick, glossy meringue. Whisk in the cornflour/cornstarch and finally, mix in the vanilla.

You can either pile the meringue on top of the jam/jelly and swirl it with a fork, or you can pipe it using a star-shaped nozzle/tip. Bake in the oven for 20–25 minutes, or until the meringue is firm and slightly golden. Serve hot with vanilla ice cream.

Christmas Pudding

Traditionally, Christmas pudding is made on 'Stir-up Sunday', when each family member takes a turn stirring the pudding mixture. It was also traditional to stir a silver sixpence into the mixture, so whoever got it in their slice on Christmas Day would be blessed with good fortune.

1 large lemon
1 carrot, grated
150 g/1½ cups fresh white breadcrumbs
50 g/⅓ cup plus 1 tablespoon self-raising/rising flour
150 g/¾ cup light muscovado sugar
1 teaspoon mixed spice/apple pie spice
½ teaspoon freshly grated nutmeg
200 g/1⅓ cups currants
200 g/1⅓ cups (dark) raisins
100 g/⅔ cup sultanas/golden raisins
150 g/1 cup ready-to-eat prunes/dried plums, chopped
250 g/8 oz. shredded beef or vegetarian suet
50 g/½ cup flaked/slivered almonds
3 eggs
150 ml/⅔ cup brandy
1 tablespoon Angostura bitters

2 x 1.2-litre/2-pint pudding basins
kitchen string
a steamer (optional)

makes 2 puddings

Line the base of each of the pudding basins with a little circle of baking parchment. You can use a pencil to trace the shape before cutting out for a good fit. Pierce the lemon all over with a sharp knife and put in a saucepan or pot of cold water. Put the lid on and bring to the boil. Uncover and simmer for about 30 minutes, or until the lemon is very soft. Drain and leave until cool enough to touch.

Cut the lemon into quarters, remove any seeds and then roughly chop. Put the lemon in a large mixing bowl along with the grated carrot, breadcrumbs, flour, sugar and spices and stir together. Add the currants, raisins, sultanas/golden raisins, prunes/dried plums, suet and flaked almonds to the bowl and thoroughly mix until everything is combined.

In a separate bowl, whisk together the eggs, brandy and bitters. Add the egg mixture to the fruit mixture and stir together.

Divide the mixture evenly between the two basins and smooth over their tops.

Cut out a 33-cm/13-in. circle from a double thickness of baking parchment. Pleat the circles and place over one pudding. Repeat for the second pudding. Cover each pudding with a lid made from a pleated circle of foil.

Wrap kitchen string twice around the basin and tie to secure the paper. Use more string to wrap over and under the bowl and tie a knot to make a handle for each pudding.

Put each basin in the top of a steamer of simmering water for 8 hours. Top up with boiling water every 1–2 hours. Alternatively, put each pudding on a trivet (or upturned ovenproof dish) in a large saucepan or pot. Add enough boiling water to come two-thirds up the side of the bowl. Cover with a well fitting lid and simmer for 6 hours, topping up the water every hour or so.

Once cool, unwrap the puddings and rewrap in baking parchment. This way you can ensure that no water has got inside. Cover each cold pudding tightly with foil and store in a cool, dark place, preferably for at least a month.

On Christmas Day, steam the pudding for 2 hours following the same method as above, then serve with flaming brandy poured over the top and generous helpings of brandy butter or cream. Merry Christmas!

Note Each pudding will serve 8–10 people. If you have a spare pudding, it can be stored somewhere cool and dark to eat the following year. Alternatively it makes a wonderful Christmas gift!

Index

Acknowledgements

Enormous thanks to my wonderful boyfriend, Richard, who was so supportive during the writing and recipe testing of this book, despite the fact his gluten intolerance prevented him from eating almost any of them. Heartfelt thanks to Nicola Carter-Lando, Susan Wilk, my little sister, Debs, and my lovely mum, for all their indispensible help with recipe testing. Thanks also to Sophie Mackenzie and Lucy Hind for their invaluable advice on South African bakes and to Sian Meades for generously lending me her Macbook charger when mine died a sudden death so close to the final copy deadline.

Thanks must go to my wonderful agent, Olivia Guest, for all her support and to the amazing team at Ryland, Peters & Small for helping to create such a beautiful book. Huge thanks to Isobel Wield for the beautiful photography and all the laughs and biscuits on portrait day and to Megan Smith for creating such a stunning design and for being so lovely to work with. Thanks also to Tony Hutchinson for his stellar prop styling and to Bridget Sargeson for her amazing food styling skills. Special thanks to Julia Charles, Leslie Harrington and Cindy Richards, and particularly my fabulous editors, Rebecca Woods and Stephanie Milner, for their excellent advice, humour and support. And lastly, a huge hug of thanks must go to my family and friends for polishing off all the mountains of test bakes – I would be so much fatter without you all.